THE NATURAL HISTORY AND BEHAVIOR OF THE CALIFORNIA SEA LION

SPECIAL PUBLICATIONS

This series, published by the American Society of Mammalogists, has been established for papers of monographic scope concerned with some aspect of the biology of mammals.

Correspondence concerning manuscripts to be submitted for publication in the series should be addressed to the chairman (and editor) of the Committee on Special Publications.

Copies of special publications may be ordered from the Secretary-treasurer of the Society, Dr. Bryan P. Glass, Department of Zoology, Oklahoma State University, Stillwater, Oklahoma 74075.

Price of this issue $3.50

Price of this issue $6.00

California sea lions: territorial bull and cows

THE NATURAL HISTORY AND BEHAVIOR OF THE CALIFORNIA SEA LION

By

RICHARD S. PETERSON
Division of Natural Sciences,
University of California, Santa Cruz

AND

GEORGE A. BARTHOLOMEW
Department of Zoology
University of California, Los Angeles

SPECIAL PUBLICATION NO. 1
THE AMERICAN SOCIETY OF MAMMALOGISTS

Published December 5, 1967

v

FOREWORD

Iɴ 1939 Seth B. Benson, then assistant curator of mammals at the Museum of Vertebrate Zoology of the University of California in Berkeley, remarked to one of us (G.A.B.) that a natural history study of the California sea lion was long overdue. Such a study was even longer overdue by the spring of 1965 when the intensive phase of our observations on this species was begun. For some inexplicable reason, during the more than quarter of a century which has elapsed since Benson's remark no detailed field study of the behavior of these most accessible of marine mammals has been published.

This neglect is remarkable in view of the wide spread interest in marine mammals which has flourished since World War II. During this period many zoologists, including the authors, have devoted much time and effort to field studies of pinnipeds in the Arctic, the Antarctic, and on remote islands, but the many thousands of sea lions which breed on the islands just off the populous coasts of southern California have been neglected. It is remarkable that the only extensive publication on the general behavior of *Zalophus californianus* is based on the isolated tropical population, *Z. c. wollebaeki*, which I. Eibl-Eibesfeldt studied in the Galapagos Islands.

We hope that our work will help to fill in an anomalous gap in the knowledge of pinnipeds, and that it will supply a background of natural history against which current and future laboratory and experimental studies of California sea lions can be interpreted. The present study is obviously little more than a first step toward understanding the social behavior of the California sea lion. Much remains to be done, particularly the quantification of information and the analysis of population dynamics. Nevertheless, even though our findings are incomplete, they should be of value as a point of departure for subsequent and more sophisticated analyses.

Our work on *Z. californianus* included the recording and physical analysis of the major patterns of vocalization in this highly vocal species, but only the more general aspects of these data are included here. The details will be published separately elsewhere.

As is the case of most field studies a number of persons and institutions contributed directly and indirectly to our research. Our field work was made possible by a grant (MH-11430-01) from the

National Institutes of Health of the U. S. Public Health Service, and by the assistance of the Marine Sciences Division of the Life Sciences Department, U. S. Naval Missile Test Center, Point Mugu, California. We are grateful for the support of Dr. C. H. Maag and Mr. F. G. Wood, Jr., of the Life Sciences Department, and of Cdr. H. R. Megrew USN and other officers and men on San Nicolas Island. We thank H. J. Chiellon, H. N. Coulombe, and E. C. Beers for their assistance in the field, and W. E. Evans and W. Ross for generously making field equipment available to us. Mr. C. H. Fiscus of the U. S. Fish and Wildlife Service has allowed us to include unpublished data from his pelagic studies of sea lions. Part of the data analysis and writing was done while one of us (R.S.P.) was a National Science Foundation Postdoctoral Fellow at the Bureau of Animal Population, Oxford University, and the other of us (G.A.B.) was aided by a grant (GB-966) from the National Science Foundation.

Oxford and Los Angeles,
June, 1966.

Contents

Illustrations

xi

INTRODUCTION

THE California sea lion, *Zalophus californianus* (Lesson) 1828, is familiar as a captive animal, but its behavior under natural conditions has been little studied. This is surprising, since it is a species which offers unusually favorable opportunities for ethological study; it is highly gregarious, relatively sedentary on land, conspicuously sexually dimorphic, locally abundant along the coasts of California and Baja California, and relatively indifferent to the presence of man. The latter characteristic is especially important since it minimizes the effect of a human observer on the social system he is attempting to study.

As Marler (1963:1081) has pointed out, the social behavior of pinnipeds is better known than that of any other wild mammals. Most of this knowledge, however, is based on three genera—the fur seals (*Callorhinus* and *Arctocephalus*) and the elephant seals (*Mirounga*). Comparative data from other pinnipeds are sorely needed, because the behavior of each of the various species is so specialized that an order-wide analysis of adequate perspective has never been possible (*cf.* Bertram, 1940). This paper undertakes to provide such information on *Zalophus*, and to make some preliminary analyses relating its behavior to that of other pinnipeds and to mammals of other orders.

Only fragmentary data are available on the natural history of *Zalophus*. Scammon (1874) gave a vivid sealer's-eye account of its status during the 19th century. Rowley (1929) presented a general account of *Zalophus* behavior (mixed with information on *Eumetopias*), but the value of his report is reduced by his undocumented assumption that the social organization of sea lions and of fur seals (*Callorhinus*) is essentially identical.

The most extensive study of *Zalophus* behavior is that of Eibl-Eibesfeldt (1955) who spent 60 hours observing the Galapagos sea lion (*Z. c. wollebaeki*). He described a number of unusual behavior

1

patterns which have not been reported in other pinnipeds: paternal care of the young (*op. cit.*:291) ; bulls' pacification of fighting females (*op. cit.*:292) ; and territorial activity of pups (*op. cit.*:294), for example.

The behavior of *Zalophus* in captivity has recently interested several investigators (Schusterman and Feinstein, 1965; Evans and Haugen, 1963) , but their experimental studies have not yet been extended into the field.

Terminology

An extensive and picturesque terminology developed for pinnipeds over the centuries of commercial hunting, and some words have become well established in scientific literature (North Pacific Fur Seal Commission, 1963) . Several of the more useful of these terms are employed in this study. A *bull* is an adult male, and a *territorial bull* is one defending an area against the intrusion of other bulls. *Pups* are young of the year, especially prior to the autumn molt. A *rookery* is a coastal area occupied by a breeding population, and a *hauling ground* is a terrestrial site occupied by non-breeding animals.

Methods

The present paper has grown out of a series of studies of the population dynamics, distribution, and behavior of pinnipeds on the islands in the Eastern Pacific during the past two decades by one of us (G.A.B.; see Literature Cited) . However, most of the data on the reproductive biology of *Zalophus* were obtained during three and a half months of intensive work on San Nicolas Island, California, during the late spring and summer of 1965. San Nicolas, the outermost of the California Channel Islands, is about 66 nautical miles southwest of Los Angeles Harbor. (For information about San Nicolas and the other islands in this group, see Hillinger, 1958, and Winslow, 1960) .

OBSERVATION.—The primary method of study was observation from a blind on a bluff overlooking a rookery on the south shore of San Nicolas Island (Fig. 1) . The behavior of individual sea lions and their social interactions were recorded in detail in a notebook at the time they were observed. Characteristic activities were recorded with both still and motion picture photography and vocalizations were recorded on a Uher 400 Report-S tape recorder. Censuses, including absolute numbers of all classes of individuals and the location and activity of marked individuals, were made on the study rookery nearly every day between 4 June and 16 September 1965. The other sea lion rookeries on the island were visited every few days. Observations were scheduled to sample all hours, day and night. During the hours of daylight we watched the animals through binoculars and a spotting telescope so that we were able to keep a large area, not only that immediately adjacent to our blind, under surveillance. Our first nocturnal observations were made with an infra-red "sniperscope," but we soon found that it was possible to crawl in among the animals at night and watch them at close range by available light. This latter method was much more instructive. We recorded nocturnal observations on a portable tape recorder, speaking quietly to avoid disturbing the animals.

MARKING.—Thirty-nine pups were marked by clipping out letters and numbers in the hair of their backs. Pups do not retreat into the sea when approached, and it was a relatively simple matter to hold them down and clip the patterns in their hair with a pair of scissors (Fig. 2). The clipped areas were paler than the rest of the pelage and the markings persisted for about three months. Eleven adult females were marked with a black aniline dye (Nyanzol D, Nyanza Chemical Co.) dissolved in hydrogen peroxide. The dye solution was placed in a projectile syringe modified by removing the needle and drilling holes around the distal end. The proximal end, containing a plunger and small explosive charge, was fitted to the head of an arrow (see Short and King, 1964). The arrows were then shot at selected female sea lions with a bow, and upon impact the dye sprayed out and made dark, irregularly shaped blotches which were still recognizable on the light brown pelage of the females after more than three months (Fig. 3). When struck by the arrow the females usually did not flee, but merely reared up and peered about as if trying to locate the source of the disturbance. This method allowed us to select specific individuals and mark them without disturbing the other animals in the rookery.

Zalophus bulls are dark brown, and the black dye proved unsatisfactory for marking them, particularly when they were wet. However, most of the territorial bulls bore conspicuous identifying scars, and we were able to identify and follow 14 of them at the study area by their patterns of scars and wounds.

Experiments in immobilizing bulls with succinylcholine chloride were undertaken as a possible aid in marking. The drug was injected through an automatic projectile syringe fastened to an arrow as described above (Fig. 4). Seven bulls were experimented on in areas remote from the study area. The paralytic dose varied from 70 to 90 milligrams. The estimated weights of these bulls ranged from 175 to 275 kg, thus, the dosage was approximately 0.25 to 0.50 mg/kg, very similar to that required for immobilizing *Callorhinus* bulls (Peterson, 1965a:692).

General Biology

Zalophus is a medium-sized otariid of marked sexual dimorphism. Adult males weigh 200–300 kg and are 200–250 cm in length, while adult females weigh 50–100 kg and measure 150–200 cm. Thus, adult *Zalophus* fall in the general size range of *Callorhinus* (Scheffer, 1958:141–142), but the difference between the male and the female is somewhat less extreme in *Zalophus* than in *Callorhinus*.

Three geographically separated populations of *Z. californianus* are recognized by Scheffer (1958) as subspecies: *Z. c. wollebaeki* in the Galapagos Archipelago, *Z. c. japonicus* in Japanese waters, and *Z. c. californianus* on the west coast of North America (see also King, 1961:218). The morphologic differences between the three populations are relatively minor.

Z. c. californianus, on which the present study is based, breeds on islands in the Gulf of California and along the west coast of Mexico south to Mazatlán, and off the Baja California and California coasts northward to San Miguel, the most northwesterly of the California Channel Islands. Non-breeding aggregations of the species occur regularly over a much wider area of the eastern Pacific, ranging as far north as British Columbia.

A conspicuous, although not complete, sexual segregation occurs in *Z. c. californianus* during the non-breeding season. The adult and sub-adult males generally move northward as soon as the summer breeding season ends, and return to the rookeries in spring. The females and young either remain in the vicinity of the breeding rookeries the year round, or, as in the case of some members of the population in the California Channel Islands, apparently move southward in winter. As a result of the differing seasonal movements of males and females, during the winter there are many females but few males in the southern half of the range of the subspecies while many males occur north of the present breeding range (Fry, 1939; Bartholomew and Hubbs, 1952; Bartholomew and Boolootian, 1960; Orr and Poulter, 1965). The seasonal segregation and migration in *Zalophus*, however, are not nearly so well defined as that of *Callorhinus* (Kenyon and Wilke, 1953).

The food of *Zalophus* consists primarily of squid, including *Loligo*, and small fish such as *Engraulis* and *Merluccius* (Bonnot, 1928; Scheffer and Neff, 1948; Fiscus and Baines, 1966). From shipboard we have seen *Zalophus* that appeared to be feeding during both day and night, but it is not known if they have a daily feeding cycle as do *Callorhinus* (Fiscus *et al.*, 1964:36) and *Leptonychotes* (M. S. R. Smith, 1965:15).

NON-REPRODUCTIVE BEHAVIOR

Locomotion

IN WATER.—The swimming of *Zalophus* resembles that of other otariids (see Howell,
1930, and Ray, 1963). The main propulsive
force is supplied by simultaneous inward and
downward strokes of the foreflippers, while
the hindflippers function primarily as stabi-
lizers or as rudders, depending upon their plane
of rotation. When turning horizontally, sea
lions extend their foreflippers and bank like a turning bird.

Contrary to statements of Rowley (1929:19), sea lions frequently
"porpoise" while swimming; that is, they leap from the water in a
shallow arc and re-enter head first. This pattern of behavior is
most common during sustained, rapid swimming. Groups of 5 to 20
young individuals sometimes swim in single file, porpoising one
after another. An intruder being chased at top speed by a territorial
bull usually porpoises while fleeing from its attacker. Young animals
often leap exuberantly out of the water during play and may
employ porpoising in play chases.

Zalophus use waves to assist them in coming ashore and going
to sea. They are skillful "body-surfers" and often glide down the
front of a wave, just submerged or partly above the surface. After
the wave breaks they ride it up to the beach, keeping their heads
and sometimes shoulders above the foam. Animals coming ashore
on a level beach usually take advantage of incoming waves, and
they ride the backwash when departing. On a steep, rocky shore,
they often utilize a wave to assist in vertical movement and may
leap from the top of the wave to land on a ledge which could otherwise be reached only after much climbing.

Aggregations of sea lions commonly sleep in the water, often in
protected areas near the shore. Sleeping animals frequently lie on
one side and elevate a foreflipper or hindflipper above the water
as described by Eibl-Eibesfeldt (1955:299), but we have never seen
them assume the "jug" posture of fur seals, that is, floating on one

side with the hindflippers and one foreflipper pressed together and held in an arch above the water. *Zalophus* is essentially a coastal animal that hauls out on shore frequently throughout the year, and as such may not need to be so well adapted to sleeping in the water as a pinniped like *Callorhinus* which remains at sea for months at a time. Furthermore, *Zalophus* may be less bouyant than the fur seals (which have thicker pelage) ; C. H. Fiscus, who has studied seals in the pelagic environment, reports (pers. comm.) that both *Eumetopias* and *Zalophus* are much more difficult to collect at sea than fur seals because the sea lions usually sink when they are shot.

On Land.—*Zalophus*, like other otariids, but unlike phocids, are capable of quite effective locomotion on land. In difficult terrain, such as among slippery rocks, an aggressive bull can probably move more rapidly than a man. Top speed across smooth rocks probably approaches 15 miles per hour, but this can be maintained for a few meters only.

Terrestrial locomotion is extremely variable, but several basic patterns can be discerned. These may be used simultaneously and in various combinations. The points of traction are the whole manus of the foreflipper and posterior portion (heel) of the hind-flipper. When moving slowly, the animals *walk*, using all four limbs alternately, much like a terrestrial quadruped. However, the hind limbs are incapable of moving independently more than a short distance and so the steps are quite short. As the animal walks, the fore and hind limbs are swung laterally as well as forward, and barely clear the ground. With each step the shoulders and hips are rotated strongly, and the head and neck swing sinuously from side to side (Fig. 5). Sometimes, when moving in a leisurely manner, a sea lion will flex the posterior half of its vertebral column laterally with each step so that the hindquarters are displaced to one side with every stride. Some individuals walking in this manner seem always to swing the hindquarters to the left, others always to the right; in a group of non-territorial bulls, we once counted 16 swinging to the left and 11 to the right.

When moving more rapidly, sea lions *gallop*, using the heels of both hindflippers as a single pivot while the foreflippers move forward slightly out of phase with each other. A galloping animal's head does not swing laterally, but bobs up and down vertically.

Galloping pups move their foreflippers simultaneously in a rapid, rotary motion.

While moving over smooth sand, going downhill, or in a few inches of water, *Zalophus* often *stride* with long steps of the fore-limbs, and drag the hindquarters limply along behind, sometimes with the hindflippers elevated slightly so that the weight rests on the abdomen. This striding pattern permits very rapid movement across wet flats or in the wash of the surf, and frequently is employed by territorial males when rushing at intruders.

An intruding bull or a submissive, estrous female will sometimes *crawl* along slowly on its belly by alternate lateral movements of its flippers, keeping the head and neck close to the ground. This crawling is somewhat like the "sinuous" locomotion of *Lobodon carcinophagus* described by O'Gorman (1963:847).

Individual Mannerisms on Land

SLEEPING POSTURES.—Sea lions have extremely flexible bodies and assume a wide variety of resting and sleeping postures while on land. Several of these are quite stereotyped and are regularly employed by individuals of both sexes and all ages. In one characteristic sleeping posture the animal lies prostrate on its belly and folds all four flippers underneath. In another, the animal lies on its side with the foreflippers against the body and the hindflippers appressed and extended to the rear. *Zalophus* also sleep sitting up on the fore-flippers, with the head thrown back and the nose pointing vertically, evidently balancing themselves comfortably in this way (Figs. 6 and 7).

GROOMING.—Despite their short sparse hair (Scheffer, 1964:293), *Zalophus* spend much time grooming, just as do marine mammals such as *Callorhinus* and *Enhydra*, which have long dense pelage. The most conspicuous and frequent grooming mannerism of *Zalophus* is a dog-like scratching with one of the hindflippers. By bending the body laterally, a sea lion can groom nearly any part of the anterior two-thirds of the body by this means. The digits of the flipper being used are flexed so that the terminal flaps fold down and the three functional claws are exposed (Fig. 8). Another common pattern of grooming involves rubbing with one foreflipper while balancing on the other; the head and neck are usually

Fig. 1. Study area on southwest shore of San Nicolas Island. See Fig. 23 for precise location.

FIG. 2. Pup that has been marked by hair clipping; grooming itself by scratching dog-fashion with hindflipper (top).

FIG. 3. Female with dye-mark on flank (bottom).

stretched upward and the palmar surface of the manus, particularly near its leading edge, is rubbed back and forth across the body. Almost the entire posterior half of the body can be reached this way. The foreflipper can also be rotated forward and used to rub the head when the neck is bent laterally. Less frequently, *Zalophus* rub their snouts across their hindquarters, and nuzzle or nibble their pelage with their incisors as dogs do.

Individuals of both sexes and all ages rub their bodies against rocks or against other animals, similar to ungulates at a rubbing post. They may also lie flat on the sand or on a smooth rock and rub their bellies or backs with lateral flexures of the body. Another characteristic grooming mannerism consists of rubbing the vibrissae against a smooth rock with a firm stropping motion, first on one side of the snout and then the other. Such "whisker-stropping" is frequently repeated by adults just after they have hauled out of the water.

EXCRETION.—Unlike most terrestrial mammals, *Zalophus* assume no special postures when urinating or defecating, nor do they pay any attention to voided wastes. They may defecate or urinate when lying prostrate or while moving about on the rookery. The frequency of defecation is good evidence that both the territorial bulls and nursing females feed regularly during the course of the breeding season.

Zalophus, particularly nursing females, sometimes vomit a white milky fluid and emit a characteristic coughing noise in the process. This regurgitation is accompanied by violent contractions of the thorax and by lateral shaking of the head; it appears to be labored and difficult.

DRINKING.—Although field observations on the drinking of sea water are always hard to verify, we saw several instances that warrant description. Territorial bulls immersed their snouts in pools of sea water and performed gulping motions, interspersed with chewing movements of the jaws after the head was lifted from the water. We do not know if water was ingested, or whether this behavior was merely mouth-wetting. We have both observed similar behavior among bulls of *Callorhinus* on warm days.

RESPONSES TO WEATHER.—Although *Zalophus* breed successfully in the tropics (in the Galapagos Islands, for example), individuals appear to be sensitive to high air temperatures and direct solar radiation. On San Nicolas Island the sky is covered with a low, unbroken overcast at least 25 per cent of the time during the summer (Winslow, 1960:30). Whenever the sky clears and direct sunlight strikes the rookeries, those sea lions not already at the water's edge arouse and move onto wet sand or into shallow water. Bulls appear to be especially sensitive, and during sunny days most of them keep thoroughly wet by frequent visits to the water. Females also go to the water's edge frequently during the day. The pups, however, are much less responsive to heat. A female that is still defensive of her new pup may drag it with her when she visits the edge of the sea or a tide pool, probably because she needs to cool off and is unwilling to be separated from her pup, not because the pup needs protection from heat.

On bright, clear days, sea lions sleeping in a prostrate position often extend their hind- and foreflippers upward and hold them motionless. By analogy with the more elaborate flipper-waving of *Callorhinus* (Bartholomew and Wilke, 1956:331, and Irving *et al.*, 1962:282), this behavior could serve to dissipate heat. But in *Zalophus*, these postures are sometimes seen on cool, overcast days, and pups also use them. Thus, we cannot be certain that a thermo-regulatory function is served. The habit of staying damp or resting on damp sand whenever heat stress exists may be sufficient in *Zalophus* to unload excessive heat. It may be significant that we have never seen behavior that we can classify with certainty as panting, even by bulls engaged in vigorous fighting.

Paulian (1964:28) suggests that the distribution of *Arctocephalus* on the windward side of Ile Amsterdam may be related to this fur seal's need for cooling. It is possible that the distribution of *Zalophus* on the Channel Islands, including San Nicolas, may be similarly related to wind direction. The great majority of the strong, steady winds on these islands are from the west and northwest (Winslow, 1960:29), and almost all the rookeries are on beaches with western exposures.

Strong winds have little effect on *Zalophus*, but if the surf is heavy the animals move inland above the breakers. Stinging sand storms occur frequently on the windward side of San Nicolas, but the animals seem indifferent to the pelting sand and allow it to drift around their bodies.

Special Senses

VISION.—The visual acuity of *Zalophus* in air is apparently limited. Even in broad daylight we were able to approach within two meters or less of aggregations of females and pups so long as we crawled slowly and kept our silhouettes low. However, a man in full view walking toward sea lions will alarm them at 75 meters or more during the day, and at 25 meters on a clear night.

When a strange object is near them (a crawling man, for example) sea lions extend their necks toward it and peer intently, swinging their lowered heads from side to side as if trying to see it better. Once when we were lying prostrate on the open beach at midday recording sea lion vocalizations, a female approached the canvas-covered tape recorder which was lying beside one of us, peered at it for about ten seconds, sniffed it, and then settled to sleep about a meter away. When the recorder clicked softly as we threw a switch, however, the animal bolted away. The sight of a man with a parka over his head, a microphone in his hand, and a recorder beside him had not been enough to cause alarm, but a simple clicking sound caused a strong flight reaction. We have had full-grown bulls actually brush against us in broad daylight while we were sitting fully exposed but with our outlines obscured by a boulder against which we were leaning.

As discussed later, *Zalophus* are as active at night as during the day, but their visual discrimination at night is even poorer than during the day. At night, by remaining close to a cliff so that we were not outlined against the sky, we were able to crawl into the aggregations of females and pups and remain for as long as we wished, so long as we did not allow the animals to sniff our faces.

However, despite their apparently poor aerial vision, sea lions readily discriminate bold outlines and rapid movements. Any bulky vertical object rising above the general level of the females' heads can cause an alarm response, especially if it moves. A vertical image of this sort is presented by a threatening territorial bull standing with elevated head and neck, as well as by a man standing up. We frequently saw aggregations of sea lions take alarm at a threatening, silhouetted bull, exactly as they would at a man approaching on foot.

The visual signals utilized by sea lions in social interactions are simple and obvious and require little more than perception of size and movement. An example is the boundary ceremony of territorial bulls, in which the head is held high and swung slowly from side to side.

Hamilton (1934:294) has described behavior in *Otaria* indicative of limited visual acuity and he suggests without further documentation that this may be related to hyper-sensitivity in bright light or to irritation of the eyes by constant wind. On the basis of ocular morphology it has been suggested that the eyes of pinnipeds are adapted for acute vision in air as well as in water (Walls, 1942:446). Although *Zalophus* may employ relatively precise visual discrimination when feeding under water (Schusterman *et al.*, 1965; Hobson, 1966), it appears that their visual discrimination in air is of a low order. Judging by their reactions to man, some pinnipeds such as harbor seals (*Phoca vitulina*) see much better in air than do sea lions.

HEARING.—The California sea lion is among the most vocal of mammals; a wide variety of vocal signals are continuously being exchanged between adults. As discussed later, the mutual recognition of mother and pup appear to depend primarily upon identification of individual vocalizations. These facts are circumstantial evidence for good hearing ability, yet *Zalophus* are relatively unresponsive to sounds such as those of aircraft or even the low conversation of humans only one to two meters distant. Sharp, sudden sounds cause immediate alarm, however, and every animal in a noisy aggregation will rise up in alarm if two rocks are struck together. They seem habituated to loud, general noises such as that of hundreds of surrounding animals and the crashing of the surf, while simultaneously discriminating and reacting to particular vocalizations of nearby individuals.

Zalophus may possess the ability to echolocate underwater (see Evans and Haugen, 1963; Poulter, 1963; Schusterman and Feinstein, 1965); this would be additional reason to suspect an acute auditory sense. From the importance of vocal signaling in their behavior on land, it seems certain that the sense is highly developed.

CHEMICAL SENSES.—Olfactory clues apparently are employed by *Zalophus* in at least two social situations on land: the interactions between males and estrous females, and in mother-pup recognition.

In the latter situation, at least, a high level of olfactory discrimination appears to be involved.

Bulls of *Zalophus* have a slight musky odor, but it is not nearly as strong as that of *Callorhinus*. We saw nothing to suggest that bulls of *Zalophus* use scent to mark their territories as has been postulated for *Callorhinus* (Peterson, 1965b:81). However, the rocks and sand of the rookeries are extremely odoriferous, as we found when crawling among the animals. It is not difficult to imagine that these smells, mostly resulting from urine and feces, could be used to recognize established hauling-out places, even when there were no other animals on shore.

Several instances of the apparent use of olfaction occurred after the carcass of a dead pup fell into a small, stagnant pool where adults had been wetting themselves frequently on warm days. On 9 June 1965, we watched a succession of bulls and females approach this pool as if about to immerse themselves in it, only to move away after sniffing at the floating carcass.

Like *Otaria* (Hamilton, 1934:295) and *Callorhinus* (authors' observations), *Zalophus* may be able at times to detect the smell of humans. On 11 June 1965, in the company of four seamen who were to assist us in marking, we approached the study area from upwind and remained completely out of sight of the sea lions. Nevertheless the entire rookery took alarm while we were more than 100 yards distant, out of sight behind a hill. It is possible that the animals detected the odor of our sweating bodies, yet during our excursions among the animals at night individual sea lions seldom took alarm until they sniffed directly and carefully at our faces. It may be that these animals are capable of discriminating various odors, and react selectively to especially strange or strong ones.

We have not seen any behavior which suggests that sea lions use their gustatory sense while on land. During hundreds of hours of observation we have never seen female *Zalophus* lick their newborn pups (*contra* Eibl-Eibesfeldt, 1955:300) and it appears improbable that taste functions in mother-young recognition in the population we studied. King (1964:124) reported that the tongue of *Zalophus* has a poor supply of taste buds.

TACTILE SENSE.—The frequency of social nuzzling and nose-rubbing in *Zalophus* suggests that the long vibrissae are highly developed sensors (Fig. 10). Vibrissal touching occurs in almost every close interaction between pairs or groups of sea lions: between females and pups, bulls and females, pairs of threatening bulls, pairs of threatening females, and among young non-breeders. The vibrissae are extremely movable and can be rotated from the folded-back resting position until they extend almost directly forward from the muzzle. We found that when curious sea lions sniffed at our faces at night, they extended their vibrissae forward and gently brushed them against us, while repeatedly opening their nostrils.

Except in the breeding season, *Zalophus* are strongly thigmotactic, and usually lie in closely packed groups, occasionally even on top of each other. At times, however, they become quite reactive to any light touch; females with newborn pups, for example, react very aggressively to even the lightest contact from another adult or pup. Thus, it appears that the skin of *Zalophus* may be quite sensitive to touch (as is that of *Monachus*, Kenyon and Rice, 1959:234), but that responses to tactile stimuli, as with those to visual, acoustic, and olfactory stimuli, are selective.

Interspecific Social Relations

The rookeries and hauling grounds of *Zalophus* are regularly visited by scavengers and are also utilized by other marine vertebrates for breeding and resting. Consequently, there are frequent opportunities for observing the relations between *Zalophus* and other species. The other pinnipeds which commonly occur in the California Channel Islands, *Mirounga angustirostris, Phoca vitulina,* and *Eumetopias jubata,* frequently share beaches with *Zalophus,* but no two of the species breed during the same season at the same location. Brandt's cormorants (*Phalacrocorax penicillatus*) sometimes breed on the same beaches with *Zalophus,* and western gulls (*Larus occidentalis*) breed immediately inland of the sea lion rookeries. The western gulls, as well as ravens (*Corvus corax*), and Channel Island foxes (*Urocyon littoralis*) scavenge among the sea lions.

ELEPHANT SEALS.—On San Nicolas Island only a few elephant seals come ashore during the sea lions' breeding season. The extensive and sustained interactions of *Mirounga* and *Zalophus* have been described elsewhere (Bartholomew, 1952:380–382), and we

have little to add here. In general, the interspecific relations of
these two species resemble the intraspecific behavior of sea lions
under similar circumstances; that is, there is a weak dominance
relationship among the non-breeders based upon individual size,
and strong territoriality among breeding bulls and parturient females. Territorial bulls of *Zalophus* threaten and chase elephant
seals that come too close, just as they would any other large animal
that approached, and even female *Zalophus* may react aggressively
toward small elephant seals. On 5 June 1965, we watched a female
Zalophus, still vigorously defending her newborn pup, threaten a
young elephant seal that was moving toward her. The elephant seal
reared up briefly as the female approached, then changed its course
and moved aside.

HARBOR SEALS.—Aggregations of *Phoca* frequently haul out on
active *Zalophus* rookeries, but harbor seals tend to remain in com-
pact groups and do not intermingle freely with the sea lions. Sea
lion bulls sometimes threaten individual harbor seals in the water
near shore, and chase them briefly. On land the harbor seals are
treated with almost complete indifference, as though they were
sea lion pups or submissive juveniles. On 20 June 1965, territorial
bull *Zalophus* were defending territories on San Nicolas area 3B
where throughout the summer aggregations of harbor seals persisted.
Whenever one of the bulls approached, the aggregations of *Phoca*
would quickly part to let him pass through, much as a pod of sea
lion pups would do. Individual sea lions and harbor seals usually
avoid contact with each other; we never saw *Zalophus* crawling
over *Phoca* as they do across each other or across *Mirounga*. But
since harbor seals move more slowly than sea lions on land, individuals of the two genera sometimes meet. When this happens, the
harbor seal usually rolls on its side, keeps its head lifted upright,
snaps its jaws at the approaching sea lion, and simultaneously makes
a rapid waving or scratching motion in the air with the uppermost
foreflipper. We never saw a harbor seal actually bite or scratch a
sea lion, but on one occasion we saw a female *Zalophus* with a new
pup viciously chase a harbor seal that had landed quietly nearby.
She dashed toward it and made a few jabbing nips at its back; the
harbor seal quickly abandoned its threatening posture and scurried
rapidly away.

Harbor seals are readily alarmed and appear to have much more acute vision than sea lions. It is, therefore, difficult for a man to approach a mixed aggregation of sea lions and harbor seals, since the harbor seals usually see him and dash for the water, and then the sea lions react by joining the stampede. The converse does not hold, for harbor seals do not react to the frequent, self-induced panics of young sea lions playing among them. When the sea lions make such a rush toward the water, the harbor seals raise their heads and look about alertly, but settle to sleep again if no danger is sighted.

STELLER SEA LIONS.—The breeding ranges of *Zalophus* and *Eumetopias* overlap at the present time only on San Miguel Island (Bartholomew and Boolootian, 1960:373), and the breeding season of *Eumetopias* occurs before that of *Zalophus*. Mixed non-breeding aggregations of the two genera are common north of the breeding range of *Zalophus* and the interactions in these groups have been described by Orr (1965a:165). The interspecific relations are generally parallel to those which occur between *Mirounga* and *Zalophus,* in that the animals tend to interact in the usual intraspecific manner.

GULLS.—Western gulls were continuously present on the sea lion rookeries, even at night. Breeding colonies of the gulls occurred within 50 meters or less of the sea lion rookeries at San Nicolas Area 1. The gulls are very bold and walk about among the sea lions quite freely, sometimes even alighting on them. They are particularly responsive to fresh placentas, and each birth attracts a noisy flock of gulls almost immediately. The gulls also eat *Zalophus* feces. They sometimes peck at the anus of a pup, following it about the rookery in their attempts.

For the most part, sea lions pay no attention to the scavenging gulls, but occasionally a female reacts to a nearby gull with an open-mouth threat. Pups and juvenile animals sometimes snap at the gulls and chase them briefly. Very young pups occasionally appear to be frightened of the gulls.

Sea lions are sensitive to sudden movements and sharp noises. Thus, any excitement among the gulls, or their alarm calls, may cause a widespread reaction among the sea lions. A single alarm call from a gull, for example, can cause one sea lion to dash toward the water, and this movement may set off a general stampede that

Fig. 4. Bow-and-arrow technique used for marking and narcotizing animals (top). See text for details.

Fig. 5. Female and pup moving from one territory to another (bottom). Note strong lateral movement of head and neck as she walks. Pup in foreground has responded to vocalizations that female directed at her own pup and is moving toward the pair.

FIG. 6. Prostrate sleeping postures of pups (top).

FIG. 7. Female sleeping in characteristic vertical posture in a semi-aquatic territory (bottom). Note territorial male in water to right of females.

will empty the beach of animals. Sometimes the birds may hover and squawk near an aggregation where there is a fresh placenta, almost as though intentionally trying to frighten the sea lions away. But the sea lions rarely react strongly to this situation. They appear to be relatively unresponsive to disturbances in the breeding rookeries during the breeding season.

MAN.—Although one can closely approach sea lions with only the most rudimentary sort of stalking, this is apparently owing to the sea lions' poor aerial vision rather than indifference to the presence of man. On the California Channel Islands, the usual reaction of sea lions as soon as they become aware of the approach of humans is a wild stampede into the water. This reaction is not invariable in the species, however. On the Galapagos Islands, individuals of the subspecies *Z. c. wollebaeki* share the indifference to man which is so conspicuous of most vertebrates of oceanic islands. At Punta Espinosa on Narborough Island in the Galapagos, some of the *Zalophus* were so unafraid of man that one of us (G.A.B.) was able to walk directly up to and touch adult females, and on one occasion was able to play tug-of-war for several minutes with a juvenile male which held a piece of driftwood in its jaws like a dog with a stick (see also Eibl-Eibesfeldt, 1955:298).

During the breeding season, the alarm reaction of the *Zalophus* in the Channel Islands population changes markedly. The withdrawal of an aggregation at the approach of a man becomes relatively slow, almost reluctant. In June and July, a territorial bull may refuse to retreat and may chase a man to its territorial boundary (Fig. 9). On 3 July 1965, we found one bull alone on a beach with the carcass of a female; this bull reacted aggressively when we approached, and refused to retreat (Fig. 10).

Similarly, females with new pups are not apt to flee from a man and will remain on the beach with their pups long after the other adults have dashed into the water. Occasionally, they even rush threateningly at a man.

Chronic human disturbance causes *Zalophus* to abandon a rookery temporarily. Our repeated efforts to mark some animals at the beginning of the study caused many females and pups to move, over a period of two days, to a new site 30 to 50 meters away. Over a period of several weeks they gradually drifted back and reoccupied the old site. If rookery disturbance persists for years, as has happened at part of San Nicolas Area 1 because of military operations, the site is finally abandoned entirely.

Zalophus are much less fearful of man in the water than on land, and they often approach swimmers and small boats closely. Groups of 15–30 young individuals (up to 3 years old) frequently rush to meet a boat and may accompany it for 100 meters or more showing every sign of excited curiosity.

Non-reproductive Social Interactions

During the non-breeding season (ap-proximately August through April), the aggregations of sea lions on land have no stable social organization. The same is also true on the hauling grounds (as con-trasted with the rookeries) throughout the breeding season. However, certain
stereotyped interactions can be seen in these unorganized groups, and the behavior follows the general patterns described in this section.

DOMINANCE RELATIONS.—There is a clear, size-related dominance relationship among non-breeders, regardless of sex. When a small individual is approached or threatened by a larger one, the smaller usually yields by scrambling aside or running, but there is no sus-tained aggressive behavior during these encounters. The hierarchi-cal relations are weak and transient, but readily apparent in any non-breeding aggregation.

GREGARIOUSNESS.—Non-breeding individuals are always highly gre-garious while on land. They often pack themselves so closely to-gether that arriving or departing animals must crawl over the bodies of the others. These congested groups form even though large sec-tions of adjacent beach remain unoccupied. The animals are strongly thigmotactic and while sleeping tend to keep their bodies pressed against each other. Even non-territorial bulls lie close to-gether in this way, especially in winter. Sometimes small individ-uals may lie on top of larger ones, but this is not tolerated for ex-tended periods of time. They also rest on the backs of elephant seals or on piles of kelp, seemingly preferring these soft resting places to rocks.

PLAY.—It is a common observation that sea lions spend much time and energy at play, both on land and at sea (see, for example, Eibl-Eibesfeldt, 1955:297). Play is difficult behavior to categorize and describe (Loizos, 1966). In sea lions, as in other mammals, play is most frequent among non-breeders, especially juveniles. The activity of pups will be described separately.

The most common pattern of play involves swimming about in the surf. An animal may ride down the front of a wave, usually just beneath the surface, until it breaks, then veer sharply to one side inside the wave, or even leap out over the crest, and then swim back out to await another wave. Sometimes several animals ride one wave together, and they may tumble over each other in the breakers. Frequently they chase each other in the water, porpoising and turning sharply. Often three or four juveniles engage in play contests over occupancy of a boulder or ledge in shallow water. One animal will climb onto the boulder and try to remain there as the others climb out of the water and try to displace it by shoving and pushing. Such contests may continue for a quarter of an hour.

Subadult males (probably sexually mature but not yet full grown) sometimes threaten each other almost as though they were on territories, using the same postures and movements as the territorial bulls. Non-breeding bulls also behave in this manner. They chase after each other, bark continually, stand chest-to-chest, push each other, shake their heads from side to side, and exchange open-mouthed threats, all of which appear to be intermediate between the play of young pups and the more aggressive interactions of territorial bulls. Wounds are not inflicted, and groups, rather than pairs, frequently participate in the skirmishes. Territorial boundaries are not maintained. For discussion of this behavior see section on ontogeny of aggressive behavior.

ALARM REACTIONS.—On the California Channel Islands, the usual alarm reaction of non-breeding *Zalophus* consists of a frantic dash for the water, even if this involves leaping off a high cliff onto a rocky beach below. The alarm is highly contagious, and usually spreads rapidly through an aggregation. If the reaction is of low intensity several animals will simultaneously rear up and look about and then gradually retreat from the direction of the disturbance, or if the disturbance is more obvious they will rush to the water's edge before stopping to look about. Sometimes hundreds of animals stampede into the water without pausing to identify the source of their disturbance. After they enter the water, they typically begin barking, form groups (rafts), and swim back toward the shore with heads held high from the water as though trying to observe the cause of their alarm.

In our experience, the immediate causes of these stampedes were human activity, alarm calls or other sudden activity of gulls, escape reactions of cormorants or harbor seals, a loud noise such as the slap of a flipper on a wet rock, or indeed any sudden movement, even that of another sea lion. Sometimes the sight of a bull standing at its full height near the inland edge of a rookery causes alarm, and on warm and sunny days the stampedes may occur for no apparent reason.

This alarm reaction is probably learned by the pups during their first few weeks of life. During their first week or so, despite their precociousness, they show no fear of man and do not join in stampedes. But by the time they are about a month old they begin to react like the adults. We have already noted that adult Galapagos sea lions show virtually no fear of man, so it is entirely possible that the alarm reaction is learned and "culturally" transmitted in the California population.

Fig. 8. Close-up of a pup scratching dog-fashion. Note that the toes are flexed to expose the claws.

Fig. 9. Territorial bull charging a man (top).

Fig. 10. Bull defending area adjacent to carcass of dead female (bottom). Note the long vibrissae and scars on the neck and chest.

REPRODUCTIVE BEHAVIOR

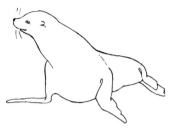

CALIFORNIA sea lions are highly polygynous; the ratio of females to
males in our study area during the
1965 breeding season averaged 14 : 1.
The typical rookery consists of territorial bulls spaced fairly uniformly in
a single line along a beach, with females in dense aggregations at irreg-
ular intervals among the bulls. This pattern of spatial organization is determined primarily by the strong gregariousness of the
females, and by the extreme aggressiveness of bulls. The arrangement of the territorial bulls depends upon the presence of females
to a large extent, although in some places the bulls defend territories on stretches of shoreline when no females are present. Most
of the unemployed males gather instead on a few separate beaches,
and on these hauling grounds they form non-territorial aggregations
similar to those that exist during fall and winter.

BREEDING SITES.—As is the case in most pinnipeds, breeding in
Zalophus tends to be restricted to a small number of the potentially
suitable localities available. Although they tend to breed on the
same sections of the coast year after year, they tend to be less
permanently fixed to traditional sites than is the case in *Callorhinus*
(Kenyon, 1960:440). For example, during the breeding season an
entire breeding aggregation of *Zalophus* may shift its location by
hundreds of meters because of repeated disturbance, sustained heavy
surf, or for no discernible reason.

On the Channel Islands, *Zalophus* usually breed on shores exposed to the prevailing winds, as discussed earlier. Rookeries exist
on both rocky shores and sandy beaches, but the locally preferred
habitat appears to be rocky flats and shelves, especially those which
are occasionally washed by large waves or submerged at high tide.
Such terrain not only keeps the animals wetted, but is frequently
cleaned of carcasses and wastes by action of the sea. At present, of
course, one of the important determinants of rookery location is the
local pattern of distribution of humans.

21

Male Territories

SHORELINE LOCATIONS.—Almost all territories of *Zalophus* bulls extend to the water's edge, a feature that affects the entire system of social organization. Access to the sea seems to be required by bulls as a part of their habit of keeping continually wetted on sunny days. Bulls that station themselves inland of the line of territories that abuts on the water are usually transient and often abandon their territories after only a few hours. Bulls sometimes establish and maintain temporary landlocked territories at night, only to abandon them in the morning. Inland bulls often are smaller and presumably younger than those in the first row along the shore, and thus may not be sufficiently large or experienced to hold a stretch of beach in face of competition from other bulls. Occasionally, tide pools are used for wetting, and a few bulls hold inland territories centered on these.

On San Nicolas Island the vertical tidal excursion is about three feet, so that the flat, sandy beaches used for rookeries are awash at high tide. Consequently, many male territories are partly aquatic. Some bulls even maintain wholly aquatic territories immediately offshore from the rookeries, staying on station in the water even when the surf is heavy (Fig. 11).

SIZE OF TERRITORIES.—The territories of *Zalophus* bulls are poorly defined. Like those of *Arctocephalus* (Paulian, 1964:96), they vary considerably between individuals, depending upon movements of females, temperature, and time of day. The specific territorial boundaries are hard to map for several reasons: (1) typically there is no inland boundary which a bull defends, (2) the seaward edge of the territory may be underwater, (3) a bull only infrequently patrols the entire perimeter of his territory, and (4) intruding bulls are sometimes tolerated in territories by the resident bull for hours at a time, very probably because he remains unaware of them. On the spacious, flat beach (Area 6B) east of our observation post, many bulls were spaced along the shore at 10- to 15-meter intervals during early June (Fig. 12); this probably represents an idealized distribution during the breeding season. On the rocky, irregular terrain that constituted our study area, six or eight territories, recognizable but irregular in shape, were usually maintained.

DURATION OF TERRITORY MAINTENANCE.—We have seen bulls defending territories during May, June, July, and August, but the territorial behavior is most intense and sustained in late June and early July, at which time some bulls even become aggressive toward humans. Although territories are maintained over a period of four months, individual *Zalophus* bulls do not stay on land continuously throughout the breeding season; in fact, few individuals remain at one location for more than two weeks. As discussed in a later section, during June and July, 1965, the duration of territory maintenance of 5 different bulls which could be individually identified from scars and marks had a mean of 9 days. Several of these bulls were seen at other places around San Nicolas Island during the summer, but at these times they were not holding territories.

Two lines of indirect evidence suggest that few bulls hold territories much longer than the individuals in our small sample: (1) the bulls do not become thin and emaciated toward the end of the breeding season as do many fur seal bulls, and (2) *Zalophus* bulls occasionally defecate on land, strongly suggesting that they are not fasting for prolonged periods.

Although the rate of turnover of bulls in the rookery is high in comparison with other polygynous pinnipeds that have been studied, the spacing and distribution of the bulls remains relatively constant throughout June and July. A new bull does not usually preempt parts of established territories; instead, it takes over the same stretch of shoreline that was held by the animal it displaced. As a result, a given territory may be occupied by a succession of different bulls during the breeding season. This contrasts with *Callorhinus* and *Mirounga* rookeries, which become progressively more crowded with bulls during the early breeding season (Peterson, 1965*b*:82; Laws, 1956:77).

ESTABLISHMENT OF TERRITORIAL STATUS.—We do not know how the first bulls in a given season establish their territorial status, but once some bulls are established, subsequent individuals must fight to gain a place. The motor activities associated with fighting appear to be aimed primarily at physically forcing the opponent out of a territory. The commonest pattern consists of chest-to-chest pushing. Quick, slashing bites and more prolonged grappling maneuvers accompany pushing, but almost always seem to be directed toward the same goal, physical displacement of the opponent. Fights occur both on land and in the water. The longest fights take place in shallow water, where the animals have greater maneuverability than on land, but where it is more difficult for a defeated animal to retreat than would be the case in water deep enough for easy swimming. Fights in deep water are very vigorous but usually brief. The defeated individual can readily escape, not only because of the agility of sea lions in water, but also because of the three dimensional nature of an aquatic territory.

Bulls on established territories bark incessantly. An intruding male, in contrast, is silent and rapidly approaches the territorial bull that it is going to attack with every indication of purposefulness but without vocalizing. A fight usually begins as soon as the intruder crosses the territorial boundary, since the established bull generally moves rapidly to meet the intruder. The ensuing fight may last several minutes. It consists of a series of violent struggles, separated by brief pauses during which the bulls stand chest-to-chest. During these pauses, the contestants hold their heads high in the air as if each were trying to tower above the other. Then, as the pause ends, each bull weaves its head and neck laterally several times and finally lunges again at the opponent's chest, flank, or foreflipper. During these lunges the animals often fall flat on their chests, necks extended. The massive, well-padded chest and the neck receive most of the wounds and seem to act as a shield for the more vulnerable flippers. If the animals are half submerged in the water, their efforts at seizing each other's flanks and foreflippers may lead them into a circular chase, sometimes with each attempting to seize the hindflippers of the other. Once a bull is bested, either by being pushed out of the territory in question, or by being overpowered and apparently losing confidence, he tries to retreat while at the same time protecting his vulnerable hindquarters. A retreating bull, therefore, repeatedly whirls to face his pursuing opponent.

A fight seldom involves more than two bulls. When the fighting pair blunders into the territory of a third bull, this neighbor sometimes attempts to bite the flipper of whichever bull he can reach. Fights involving several bulls at their territorial intersects, as seen in *Callorhinus* (Bartholomew and Hoel, 1953:484; Peterson, 1965*b*:67), were never observed in *Zalophus*. This probably is a function of the lower level of aggressiveness, and rather indefinite

FIG. 11. Two bulls maintaining adjacent territories in the water at one edge of study area.

FIG. 12. Typical spatial arrangement in a rookery on a sandy beach with animals on damp sand at water's edge. Territorial bulls are spaced at intervals of 10 to 15 meters, and the confluent female aggregations are arranged without reference to the boundaries of male territories.

territorial boundaries of *Zalophus* as compared with *Callorhinus*.

MAINTENANCE BEHAVIOR.—Once a bull is established on territory, it does relatively little fighting. A territory rarely borders more than two or three others, and established neighbors are not concerned with displacing each other, but merely with maintaining their own territories. Territorial maintenance activities consist primarily of loud and frequent vocalizations, and of displays with formalized postures and movements. The loud and incessant barking of a territorial bull continuously advertises his presence and broadcasts his intent to defend his territory. When not aimed at any specific bull these barks are relatively slow, but if the territorial bull is moving toward another male, the rate of barking increases, apparently signifying a more intense and directed threat.

Pairs of established bulls regularly perform a stereotyped *boundary ceremony*, reaffirming their mutual territorial limits. They rush toward each other, barking rapidly, with vibrissae extended anteriorly. Just before reaching the boundary between their territories they stop barking and fall on their chests, open their mouths widely, shake their heads rapidly from side to side, and weave their necks laterally at a rate much slower than the head-shaking which is simultaneously going on. They then rear themselves to maximum height, twist their heads sideways, and stare obliquely at each other. Three stages of this ceremony are shown in Figures 13, 14, and 15. The process is ritualized, and the animals do not touch each other; if they happen to be unusually close together they skillfully avoid contact. Sometimes during the boundary ceremony the two bulls partially cross the boundary and stand side by side, facing opposite directions, making feinting jabs at the chest and flippers of each other. The oblique stare is often the last component of the display prior to the bulls' separation, or prior to repetition of the entire head-shaking, neck-weaving sequence.

TEMPORARY INTRUDERS.—The activities associated with territorial maintenance by established bulls are not continuous. Periods of alertness and movement are interspersed with intervals of sleep, often at apparently preferred sites within the territory. During these intervals of male inattention, which may last for several hours, neighboring territorial bulls show no interest in entering the untended territory. Non-territorial, wandering bulls, however, often move cautiously into a territory at such times, usually "hiding" among the resident females. These intruders may be fully grown, or they may be small animals the same size as the females. They usually approach from the landward side, having landed at some undefended place and wandered inland to the rookery, although sometimes they enter from the sea. They do not vocalize, nor do they challenge or otherwise disturb the bulls in adjacent territories. Often they show sexual interest in the females, and may attempt to mount them. When one of these intruders is discovered by the resident bull, a vocal threat is ordinarily enough to send him rushing away. Sometimes the intruder remains undiscovered for hours, and we observed one that remained quietly (apparently unnoticed) in a territory for three days. Intruders seem to remain undetected as long as they are visually inconspicuous and do not respond with threatening or rapid movements to the activity of the resident bull. Thus, there is a premium on their behaving very much like females. Perhaps because of poor aerial vision bulls do not readily recognize these intruders as males.

Early in the breeding season, most of the temporary intruders are fully grown bulls, evidently from the hauling grounds. Toward the end of the season, they are more often young males about the size of the females. A corresponding decrease in the number of adult males on the hauling-ground population occurs as the season progresses. If fully grown and allowed to remain for many hours without being challenged by the resident bull, a temporary intruder may gain enough confidence to stand its ground briefly and return the threat of the resident. But although they sometimes fought with the resident, we never saw the temporary intruders successfully establish themselves as territorial bulls.

The frequency of these intrusions is surprisingly high, evidently because the linear arrangement of the territories makes almost every territory accessible to wandering animals from both the landward and the seaward sides. During the period between 1100–1400 hours, 14 June 1965, we saw four temporary intruders enter seven territories at the study area. Later in the season, small males sometimes dashed into the aggregations of females every few minutes, frequently unnoticed by the resident bulls, and often unnoticed by us until they bolted from among the females when the resident threatened them.

Because these temporary intruders are transient, and almost never defend their positions, we do not consider the territories to be composite, nor the intruders to be "subordinate breeding males" as in *Mirounga* (Bartholomew, 1952:394; Carrick *et al.*, 1962:173).

RELATIONS OF FEMALE AGGREGATIONS TO MALE TERRITORIES.—The individual females on a rookery pay no attention to the territorial boundaries maintained by the bulls. The bulls patrol the boundaries irregularly and make no effort to herd females into their territories or to hold them there. Consequently the arrangement of the female aggregations shows no regular relationship to the territories of the males, nor is a given female confined by a bull to any one territory. Therefore, the word "harem," so firmly established in the literature on pinniped behavior, is not applicable to *Z. c. californianus*. Eibl-Eibesfeldt (1955) uses the German term *Herd*, suggesting harem, for the Galapagos sea lion.

Although the females are relatively independent of bulls' territories, the converse does not hold. Stable and organized territories exist only when and where females are present, and shifts in the females' locations modify the territorial activities of the bulls. Such shifts in the locations of the females occur erratically, with storms or disturbances, and regularly, with the tidal and day-night cycles. The tidal cycle in California has a duration of approximately 12 hours; the females generally stay near the water's edge, shifting back and forth on the beach with the tide. The territorial bulls generally move back and forth with them; the lateral and seaward boundaries of the territories are fixed but the inland boundaries are less definite. At night, the females usually move back to the inland edge of the beach and sometimes even go above the beach onto vegetation-covered terraces. The territorial bulls tend to accompany the female groups as they move inland at night, though they still continue to defend the seaward edges of their territories. If the females abandon a stretch of shore completely, as they sometimes do in the face of a heavy surf, the bulls remain on the vacant beach for only a day or so before deserting their territories. Occasionally, however, one finds a stretch of shore on which bulls are widely spaced and aggressive toward each other even though females have not been ashore there. We do not know how long bulls maintain their stations in such areas, or why they are aggressive there, but not aggressive on the hauling grounds.

NOCTURNAL ACTIVITY.—We frequently visited the rookeries and hauling grounds at night, and on 30 June 1965 we maintained an all-night watch at the study area. In the rookeries, activity was, if anything, greater at night than during the day. Although some of the females and many of the pups slept, sleeping seemed no more common at night than during the day. All of the usual activities seen during the day also took place at night. Vocalizing continued unabated. Some females went to sea; others returned to suckle their pups. Pups played, wandered about, slept, or suckled. The territorial bulls were somewhat more active at night than during the day. They moved about more continuously and appeared more zealous in their inspection of females and their chases of intruding males. It seems probable that the heightened level of activity of the bulls at night is associated with the fact that over-heating is not as acute a problem at night as it is during the day.

In contrast to the situation on the rookeries, the level of activity on the hauling grounds frequented by the non-territorial males was much lower at night than during the day. Most of the animals on the hauling grounds moved inland and slept.

Behavior of Females

GREGARIOUSNESS.—The polygynous social order of this species results from two basic elements, the male territory and the female aggregation, both of which vary seasonally as do the relative aggressiveness and the relative gregariousness of male and female. Arriving pregnant females are clearly attracted  to the vicinity of other females already on land. Although just after parturition the heightened aggressiveness between females produces a quasi-territorial pattern among them, one rarely sees a female-pup pair isolated by itself. Almost always the females remain in aggregations, albeit at the height of pupping the aggregations become rather loose. Later in the season the aggressiveness between females diminishes markedly and the females and their pups are nearly always found concentrated in aggregations. It should be emphasized that throughout all of the female's activity, some degree of gregariousness persists.

FIG. 13. Figures 13, 14, and 15 show typical patterns of movement in the boundary ceremony of adjacent territorial bulls. In this photograph the animal on the left has just lunged forward and both animals are shaking their heads from side to side.

Fig. 14. Boundary ceremony continued; the oblique stare

ARRIVAL AT THE ROOKERY.—Pregnant females apparently land at the rookery only a day or so before giving birth. They are noticeably bulky, walk with relative difficulty, and are restless and irritable. Sea lions are conspicuously vocal, but the pregnant females are very quiet and rarely if ever vocalize.

The bulls generally pay little attention to the individual females as they accumulate on the rookery, but sometimes they bark at them and approach and sniff at their noses. Infrequently, a bull will attempt to nuzzle a newly arrived female's flanks or rump. The females generally ignore or avoid the bulls, but sometimes they react to the approach of a bull with open-mouthed threats or by retreating. Only infrequently do bulls attempt to "herd" females into their territories by threatening or blocking their way. When it does occur, such behavior is much less vigorous than that of *Callorhinus* bulls (Bartholomew, 1953). We never saw *Zalophus* bulls make either prolonged or effective efforts to retain females in their territories. Usually a territorial bull gives no response to arriving or departing females, even if in full view of the bull. In this species we saw nothing which we could interpret to be a "harem."

AGGRESSIVENESS BETWEEN FEMALES.—Even though they are gregarious and almost always gather in groups, a conspicuous feature of the behavior of *Zalophus* females during the the breeding season is their aggressiveness. As mentioned above this aggressive behavior is heightened considerably at the time of birth when parturient females are virtually territorial (*cf.* Eibl-Eibesfeldt, 1955:293).

Most of the aggressiveness of the females is quite formalized and despite its vigor and noisiness injuries are rarely inflicted. Typically, an aggressive female shifts about restlessly near her pup, barking continually and rushing toward any neighbor that approaches too closely. She threatens by extending her neck and twisting her head to one side with mouth open wide. The female being threatened responds in a similar manner. Thus, one often sees pairs of females weaving their heads and necks back and forth and vocalizing (Fig. 16). Sometimes the two animals freeze in this head-aside posture for several seconds. If the contest is not terminated at this stage, they may begin biting each other on the necks or flanks and sometimes they roll and writhe on the ground like wrestlers, but inflict no wounds. Finally, one of the individuals withdraws a few feet and the squabble dies away. These inter-actions are very common and, since they disturb adjacent females, tend to be contagious. Sometimes three or four, or even more, fe-males become involved. But the aggressive displays are brief (a minute or less) and usually result in nothing more than minor shifts of location. If the aggregation is startled, as by the alarm call of gulls, the resulting changes in position of the females stimulate a great many aggressive interactions.

We have seen no evidence of stable dominance hierarchies, as occur in *Mirounga* females (Bartholomew and Collias, 1962:8). The absence of such hierarchies may be related to the greater mo-bility of *Zalophus* and the resultant decrease in numbers of con-tacts between the same individuals; *Mirounga* females lie almost immobile near each other for several days. Transient dominance-subordinance relations between pairs of *Zalophus* females do occur: pregnant females, females without pups, or females *en route* to the sea usually behave subordinately.

AGGRESSIVE VOCALIZATIONS.—There are at least four vocalizations associated with the inter-female aggressive behavior. The com-monest is the *bark* which is similar to that of the bull but higher pitched. It identifies and localizes a female and serves as a relatively mild, long-distance threat. When two contesting females are close together, three intergrading vocalizations are used. The least in-tense of these is a *squeal* which is of variable pitch, sometimes quite high. It is made with wide-open mouth and usually accompanies the head-weaving behavior sequences. The *belch* is a somewhat more intense threat, a prolonged, harsh, gagging sound, usually accompanied by forward thrusting of the head. The most intense vocal threat is an irregular *growl* which has a harsh, erratic, aspirate quality and is often used during actual strikes with the head or during biting.

"PEACE-KEEPING" BY BULLS.—The noisy squabbles of females some-times evoke a response from the nearest territorial bull which begins to bark loudly, moves rapidly toward the females involved, and may attempt to sniff or nuzzle them. Eibl-Eibesfeldt (1955:292) inter-preted this behavior in the Galapagos sea lion to mean that "Das Männchen duldet keinen Streit unter den Herdenmitgliedern" and suggested further that bulls actively prevent females from fighting.

Steller (1751; translation:203) ascribed similar meaning to the reactions of fur seal bulls to squabbles in their territories.

We saw nothing in our study to which we would apply such interpretations. Bulls react in a similar "peace-keeping" manner to any disturbances within their territories. For example, to young intruding males or especially noisy pups at play. It is reasonable to assume that this response of bulls is simply a general reaction to heightened activity in their territories. The bull's approach may temporarily halt the fighting between females, by frightening them into fleeing a short distance, but it certainly does not pacify them.

Parturition

Our daily censuses indicate that most of the pups were born during June. Pregnant female sea lions are easily recognized by their distended abdomens and laborious locomotion. Although we watched them carefully throughout the pupping season we witnessed only two deliveries, one at 1715 hours on 20 June, and one at 1900 hours on 22 June 1965. Since new pups were present on the rookery almost every morning during the pupping season, we conclude that most deliveries occurred at night.

During parturition, the females became increasingly restless as they passed through the first stage (vaginal dilation) and frequently turned to nuzzle the perineal region, sometimes circling about like a dog chasing its tail. During this stage both the females we observed uttered a few, brief *pup-attraction calls* (see section on mother-young recognition), but otherwise were silent. This vocalization was directed toward the perineum, as if in anticipation of delivery.

Both deliveries were by anterior (cephalic) presentation (*cf.* Slijper, 1956:42). In one birth which was timed, the second stage lasted 2.5 minutes. More than two minutes were required for the pup's head and shoulders to appear, and then movement was rapid as the thorax, the thickest part of the spindle-shaped fetus, was delivered. Thereafter, the hindflippers appeared almost immediately. The umbilical cord was broken, in both cases, by the time the pups were delivered. The third stage (placental delivery) occurred after 17 minutes in one case, and did not take place for at least one hour in the other case.

The new pups lay on the rocks quivering for a few seconds, then began to struggle weakly, made feeble attempts to stand on their foreflippers, and succeeded in doing so within a minute or so. They shook themselves like dogs several times during the first few minutes, just as wet adults do, and soon began vocalizing.

Courtship and Copulation

Females come into estrus about two weeks after parturition. The vulva of an estrous female becomes pink and slightly edematous, and is therefore much more conspicuous than in other females.

COURTSHIP.—Territorial bulls are relatively inactive in courtship. They do not examine the females that happen to be in their territories with any regularity or system. However, bulls often attempt to sniff the noses of females that are moving about, and will nuzzle persistently at the genital area of any female that is lying prone and is at all receptive. Sometimes a bull will move about a female, barking and shaking his head, much as in the formal aggressive encounters between males. When used in courtship, however, this behavior assumes a rather tentative quality and may culminate in the bull's rubbing his whiskers along the female's body and nipping at her shoulders and sides (Fig. 17). Such a courtship performance by the bull is by no means invariable and is always less vigorous than in *Callorhinus*.

When a *Zalophus* female comes into estrus she usually solicits the male to mount her. This contrasts sharply with other pinnipeds in which the male plays the active role. The *Zalophus* female approaches the bull, and by characteristic submissive postures and languorous movements (*estrous display*) invites sexual attention. An estrous female lies prone in front of the bull, on her side, belly, or back, and repeatedly presses her body against his. She executes slow, writhing movements on the ground, rubbing against the bull, stretching, and looking up at him. Sometimes while making these twisting movements she slithers across the back and shoulders of the male, almost as though mounting him. Usually, but not invariably, the male soon begins sniffing at her genital region. She responds by arching her back upwards and spreading her hind-flippers. The male generally mounts after a few minutes, though sometimes courtship continues for an hour or longer.

FIG. 15. Boundary ceremony continued; elevated posture with head shaking

Fig. 16. Open-mouthed threats by females

COPULATION ON LAND.—In copulation the female lies prone, usually on her belly, and the bull mounts her from the rear. The front limbs of the male are short and the female is relatively large, so even when the bull supports himself on his foreflippers, his chest and belly rest on the female (Fig. 18). Occasionally a bull rests his entire weight on the female and clasps her with his foreflippers. The bull's pelvic thrusts are intermittent. He usually mounts and dismounts the female several times before copulation is terminated. Between mountings the female resumes estrous display. The male may cover her when she is lying on her side or even on her back and make pelvic movements. These copulatory activities, including mountings during which the pair rub their necks together, may continue for an hour or more and the pair may even fall asleep for a few minutes while lying on or against each other. We were unable to tell whether or not intromission occurred during all the mountings. In all instances observed, copulation was actively terminated by the female; she raised her head and forequarters, bit at the neck of the male and pulled free, even though the bull was often still making pelvic movements.

Once a copulation has been terminated by the female, her behavior changes abruptly. She rebuffs the approach of her former partner or other sexually interested males with jerky, spasmodic movements of the head, not seen at other times, and also actively retreats from them. We never saw a given female carry out more than one series of estrous displays, nor participate in more than one prolonged copulatory series, nor remain sexually active after a completed copulation. However, if the first male solicited by an estrous female is lethargic or unresponsive, she sometimes moves to an adjacent territory and directs her displays at the male there. In one case a male repeatedly mounted a female over a period of about 1½ hours, but for some reason his activities were inadequate. The female then moved to another bull in an adjacent territory and courtship and copulation continued for an additional 15 minutes before she became unreceptive.

For the most part sea lions show no response to or apparent interest in the behavior of a sexually active pair. Once (13 July 1965), however, we observed a female swim up to a pair which were copulating in the water, sniff at the head of the male, and then nip him gently first on the flank and then on the neck. He made no response other than to sniff at her nose when she approached. On another occasion (4 July 1965), two females on land were simultaneously courting the same territorial bull. During a period of about half an hour he repeatedly mounted each female, sometimes lying across both of them at the same time. Finally, he completed a copulation with one of the females which then bit him on the neck, pulled free and moved rapidly away. The male followed her for about 10 meters, but she rebuffed him with the spasmodic head movements referred to above. After about three minutes the male returned to the second female who promptly resumed her sexual displaying. The male mounted her and copulation proceeded. After 5 minutes the second female bit the neck of the male and pulled free and moved away. The male did not follow her.

During a prolonged courtship, a bull may leave the female and exchange vocal threats with another bull, but he becomes relatively unresponsive to his neighbors while he is sexually engaged. Sexual behavior takes precedence over aggressive behavior; we never saw a bull interrupt copulation to engage in aggressive interactions with another bull.

COPULATION IN THE WATER.—Since many bulls' territories are partly aquatic, and since females usually stay near the water's edge, copulation often begins when the two animals are partly in the water. If in shallow water, copulatory behavior follows the same general sequence as on land, except that the female rests on the bottom under water and must occasionally lift her nose to the surface to breathe.

We also observed a number of copulations in deep water, where neither the male nor the female was in contact with the bottom. Courtship, usually brief, is similar to that on land except that the animals are swimming. To mount, the bull clasps the female with his foreflippers, holding her against him. The pair sometimes roll over in the water, float on their sides, or sink entirely under water and wash back and forth in the surge, breathing only intermittently. Judging from its frequent occurrence and duration, aquatic copulation appears to be successful in *Zalophus*, a point that has been much argued for *Callorhinus* (Bering Sea Tribunal of Arbitration, 1895).

MOTHER–YOUNG RELATIONS AND ONTOGENY OF PUP BEHAVIOR

Perinatal Behavior

PINNIPEDS are among the most precocial of mammals (Nice, 1962:17) and *Zalophus* conforms to this generalization. The pups have their eyes open at birth and within 10 to 15 minutes after delivery they can carry out highly coordinated motor activities. For example, a newborn pup can shake itself like a wet dog, scratch with the hindflippers, rub its flanks with the foreflippers, and use its incisors to nibble and groom the pelage. Walking becomes coordinated within the first 30 minutes. Vocal interchanges with the mother begin at birth, and the pup almost immediately develops the capacity for effective vocal communication.

POST PARTUM MOTHER-YOUNG INTERACTIONS.—Shortly after delivery, the female begins nuzzling her newborn pup, rubbing her vibrissae over it and (perhaps incidentally) brushing away bits of fetal membrane that may be sticking to its pelage. She repeatedly lifts the pup to her side with her teeth and nips at its body. Although this nipping and nuzzling continued for at least 10 minutes, we never observed a female lick her pup (*contra* Eibl-Eibesfeldt, 1955:295), nor eat the fetal membranes or placenta.

Immediately after birth the pup and its mother begin an initial series of vocal interchanges, which continue for 15 to 20 minutes with little pause. The females make a bawling, trumpet-like *pup-attraction call* and the pups respond with the *mother-response call*, a quavering vocalization reminiscent of the bleat of a lamb. As indicated previously, in the two births which we observed the females began to utter the pup-attraction call shortly before the pup was delivered. During the first several hours, these vocal interchanges between pup and female are repeated a number of times. In the intervals between these vocal interchanges the pair spends much of the time sleeping. This post partum vocal interchange anticipates

35

the pattern of vocalizing that takes place between a female and her pup when they are re-uniting to suckle after separation. Thus, it may help establish the mutual recognition of mother and young (see Collias, 1956, for a discussion of this problem in sheep).

We were surprised to observe that parturient females are nearly as attentive to their neighbors as to their newborn pups. They bark vigorously and make frequent, threatening dashes at adjacent animals. We saw one female leave her pup as soon as it was delivered and rush over and threaten a neighbor, before returning to nuzzle her pup for the first time. This aggressive, almost territorial, behavior seems to have priority over all other activities at this stage, even over preliminary interactions with the pup.

MOTHER-YOUNG, DURING FIRST FEW DAYS.—Females are very protective of their pups for the first two to four days, and may even refuse to leave them if approached by a man. Physical contact between mother and young is maintained almost continuously, the female repeatedly tugs or lifts her pup to her side by the loose skin of its nape and shoulder region whenever she shifts position slightly or the pup starts to wander away. If sufficiently disturbed, by weather or human activity, a female with a new pup will carry or drag it in her mouth to a new location. Sometimes this involves carrying the pup to sea. On 7 June 1965 we watched a female drag her pup by its nape, first to the shore and then out into the surf for perhaps 50 meters. The pup struggled frantically whenever released from the female's mouth, and several times it tried to crawl onto her shoulders in a manner similar to that described by Kenyon (1956). The female repeatedly caught the pup and lifted it above the surface. Twelve minutes after entering the water, they drifted to shore about 400 meters distant from where they started. The female helped the pup through the surge and onto the beach, and finally the pair joined a group of females and pups in the new area.

Similar shifts in location occur on land. When a pup is less than a week old, the female may carry or drag it; otherwise it follows along behind her, vocalizing repeatedly. In a few unusual cases, we observed females continuing to carry their pups cat-fashion when 2–3 weeks of age. If the move involves climbing over rocks or ascending ledges, a female tugs roughly at her pup and may drop it several times. Partly as a result of this treatment, many young pups have scratches and lacerations on their napes, although

FIG. 17. Neck-rubbing prior to copulation (top). Note conspicuous size difference between male and female.

FIG. 18. Typical copulatory posture (bottom). This picture was taken shortly after Fig. 17.

Fig. 19. Pups playing in shallow water near shore

the scratches may also result from forceful rebuffing by other females. As pointed out previously, the female aggregations gradually
shift position with the tide and daylight, sometimes moving 30–50
meters on a flat, open beach. During these slow changes in location
the pups usually follow their mothers without being carried.

On sunny days when overheating is a problem, females make repeated trips to tide pools or the edge of the sea, sometimes every
hour or so, and get themselves wet. If pups are less than a week old,
the females take them along and drag them into the water. The
pups flounder to shore and try to crawl out on land, but the females,
apparently reluctant to be separated from their pups, pull them
back into the water. This pattern, which appears to involve a
combination of behavioral thermoregulation and mother-young ties,
is probably the basis for the familiar folk belief that sea lions teach
their pups to swim. On first sight, it does appear quite like a "swimming lesson."

Sometime during the first day, the pup starts to suckle. As
pointed out by Eibl-Eibesfeldt (1955:296), there is no stereotyped
teat-searching behavior in *Zalophus* pups. Newborns nuzzle about,
apparently at random, until they find the site of one of the retracted
nipples, although later they learn to locate the site rapidly.

After approximately four days, the females no longer remain
continually with their pups. At first, separations may be very brief,
but as the season progresses, the females spend more time at sea,
and the pups begin to wander about the rookery, depending on
their mothers only for nutrition and not for protection.

Pup Behavior

The terrestrial locomotion
of pups during their first
months is much less variable
than that of the adults, consisting of only two patterns: a
slow *walk*, and a faster *gallop*.
Both patterns are employed
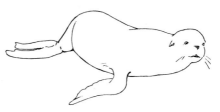
shortly after birth, but pups become noticeably more agile as the
weeks progress.

Pups apparently can swim at birth, but their first efforts are
awkward, consisting of rapid rotary movements of the forelimbs

while the head is held high above the water. This pattern is strikingly similar to the terrestrial *gallop*, which also employs simultaneous rotary movements of the foreflippers. Swimming skill develops rapidly. Breathing coordination and use of the flippers improves steadily and by mid-July many of the pups spend long periods in the water (Fig. 19).

Pups spend much of their time sleeping. Their sleeping postures (Fig. 6) are similar to those of adults. If the terrain is flat the sleeping pups orient themselves randomly, but on a slope they tend to lie with heads uphill.

By mid-June, when many of them are two to three weeks old and their mothers are no longer in continuous attendance, the pups begin to aggregate in groups. Thereafter, these pods of pups become a progressively more conspicuous feature of the rookery. Pups are very gregarious: if one becomes isolated while sleeping, its first act upon awakening is to rush frantically to the nearest pod. The pup pods may include as few as 5 or 6 or as many as 200 individuals. The composition of a given pod is always in a state of flux; individuals and small groups frequently join it or move away, and occasionally the entire group moves off to a new location.

Typically, these pods are located near the female aggregations, and shift with them diurnally and tidally. Pups aggregate in areas where the territorial activity of the bulls is minimal. Thus, they accumulate on the edges of the rookeries, among large boulders, or beneath overhanging ledges. Bulls pay little attention to pups, although sometimes it appeared that a bull would slow somewhat before rushing through a pod, permitting the young to scramble out of his way. We saw very few pups run over by bulls.

Pups appear to be less sensitive to heat and more sensitive to cold than adults. They show no tendency to keep continually wetted on warm days, and unlike adults, when they are wet, they often shiver and repeatedly shake water from their pelage. From these responses we infer that the young animals are poorly insulated and dissipate heat readily, as is the case with *Callorhinus* pups (Bartholomew and Wilke, 1956:331; Irving *et al.*, 1962:276).

Pup Vocalization.—The only vocalization produced by newborn pups is the bleating *mother-response call*, but after they become older and form pods, they begin to use three other intergrading vocalizations. If a pup is struggling, as during play, it occasionally emits an explosive, unvoiced *cough,* or a rapid series of them which sometimes become voiced. If a pup becomes agitated, it often prolongs the voiced portion of the series, and produces a relatively high-pitched *alarm call.* In early August, when many pups are about six weeks old, they begin to develop the adult-like *bark,* a threat which seems to arise as a segmented version of the alarm call.

All three of these vocal patterns have social significance, evoking various responses from nearby pups and adults. We shall discuss vocalization further in a separate paper.

PLAY OF PUPS.—The play of sea lion pups resembles that reported for northern fur seals (Bartholomew, 1959). From the time a pup first joins a pod it engages frequently in elaborate play behavior which appears to have no immediate relevance to nutrition, reproduction, or protection, but may adumbrate adult behavior.

Individual pups exhibit many playful motor patterns: rocking laterally from one foreflipper to the other, rolling onto the back and waving the flippers in the air, and elevating the forequarters while simultaneously bending the neck back sharply and peering about over the back.

Most of the pups' play is social, however. Sometimes two or three pups rub their heads, necks, and bodies together, rotate their vibrissae forward, and touch noses. They often nip each other's faces and forequarters, or gently interlock jaws. Some of these activities assume the stereotyped configurations of adult aggressive interactions. For example, open-mouthed threats, feinting lunges at flippers and necks from a prone posture (Fig. 20), and mounting with sketchy copulatory movements are frequently seen.

Sometimes large groups of pups engage in contagious patterns of play. A pod may travel *en masse* through the rookery, moving erratically and without regard to the bulls' territories. One or two pups often appear to lead these mass movements temporarily, while the others gallop along behind, frequently stopping to nip each other or roll on the ground in a brief scuffle. These wandering groups seem to be attracted to conspicuous objects in the rookery such as dead animals or tide pools.

By the time pups are about six weeks old they make short exploratory trips inland from the rookery singly and in small groups, sniffing and rubbing against boulders, plants, or concealed human observers. As the season progresses they wander more and more widely, venturing along the coast and out to sea for short distances. By late July the tide pools and sheltered inlets in the vicinity of the rookery are often filled with bobbing pups, engaged in protracted and elaborate aquatic play (Fig. 19). They submerge their heads, peer about under water and chase each other over partially submerged cobbles and boulders, frequently touching or nipping each other. We watched one pup that seemed quite entertained by immersing its muzzle repeatedly and blowing streams of bubbles from its nostrils.

Pups also play with inanimate objects. They are strongly attracted to pieces of the giant kelp (*Macrocystis*) which commonly wash ashore, and they endlessly shake and toss them about. Several pups may successively play with the same piece of kelp, and occasionally two may tug on a piece at the same time. Small pebbles and sticks are also picked up and held in the mouth, although we never saw them thrown, as Eibl-Eibesfeldt (1955:297) describes for *Z. c. wollebaeki*. Some pups energetically gnaw at rocks or banks, occasionally packing their mouths full of sticky sand.

Mother–Young Recognition and Suckling

SUCKLING.—A pup soon learns the location of its mother's four retractable teats and switches from one to another as it suckles (Fig. 21). The nipples emerge during suckling; whether extruded actively or passively we could not determine; within a few seconds after a pup releases a nipple, it retracts. The process of suckling is surprisingly noisy, and smacking noises can easily be heard from a distance of 10 meters. As Eibl-Eibesfeldt (1955:296) has described in *Z. c. wollebaeki*, the pups use suction to obtain milk, rather than massaging the teat with the tongue as some mammals do. Except for lying on her side and exposing the area of the teats, the female does not appear to assist the suckling pup; frequently she sleeps while the pup feeds.

The usual pattern is for a pup to suckle steadily, with short breaks, for about one-half hour, and then separate from its mother. The mean, minimum, and maximum of five periods of suckling, timed during daylight hours on 17 July 1965, were 33, 20, and 48 minutes. After such a period, the pup appears to be satiated and wanders away from its mother. We seldom saw a pup which was more than two or three weeks old engage in more than one such suckling period in a single day, but very young pups may suckle intermittently for several hours. As discussed in detail later, pups reunite with their mothers and feed at irregular intervals, seldom more often than once each day or less frequently than once a week.

MAINTENANCE OF MOTHER-PUP TIES.—We were able to mark four female-pup pairs shortly after parturition (judged by fresh placentas or by witnessing birth), and we saw these pairs reunite repeatedly during the three months following. We never observed among these eight individuals any suckling which did not involve a mother and her own pup. We also kept records of a number of other female-pup pairs which although not marked immediately after parturition were assumed to be mother and young because of the female's attentiveness and the fact that she suckled the pup. We never saw a female suckle any but her own pup nor did we see any female accept two pups, either simultaneously or successively. Therefore, we conclude that a *Zalophus* female recognizes her own individual pup and nurses it to the exclusion of all others. Similar integrity of the mother-young bond has been described for *Callorhinus* (Bartholomew and Hoel, 1953:420–21) and *Mirounga* (Bartholomew, 1952:391), although fosterage frequently occurs in *Halichoerus* (E. A. Smith, 1965:73–74).

Mother-young recognition probably becomes mutual by the time a pup is about two months old, but prior to this, the integrity of the pairs appears to depend on the female. Young pups respond positively to any searching female, but the female rebuffs all pups but her own. The usual rebuff is an open-mouth threat but sometimes the female seizes the pup in her teeth and tosses it randomly into the air. This maneuver is usually performed awkwardly and sometimes the pup is thrown against the female instead of away from her. The rejection is obvious, however, and the pup always retreats rapidly.

MOTHER-YOUNG RECOGNITION.—When a female comes ashore and starts searching for her pup, she vocalizes repeatedly, approaches any pups which respond, and appears to examine them both olfactorily and visually. When she finds the proper pup the process of mutual identification generally takes only a minute or two, and suckling begins shortly thereafter. Since the reuniting of mother and pup usually takes place before the female has been ashore long enough for her pelage to dry out (5–15 minutes), we infer that this behavior has a high priority when a female returns from feeding at sea.

A rookery may contain hundreds of females and pups. The probable clues by which females and pups might identify each other individually are few. Because we could not perform experiments without disturbing the group we were studying, we have attempted to assess the relative importance of several probable recognition factors by repeated observations of the process under undisturbed conditions.

1) *Geographic location*: Neither females nor pups appear to be tied to a particular geographical site. Newborn pups may be moved from one place to another by their mothers; older pups move with their mothers for long distances, and the reunion and suckling of a given pair occur at different sites at different times. From these facts we conclude that *strict* geographic localization within the rookery is not a primary factor in bringing a *Zalophus* female and pup together, and that there is no one place to which a given pair returns for reunion. Geographic localization could, however, offer an important preliminary clue if, after each trip to sea, the female returned to the approximate site at which she last suckled her pup. Such a pattern would allow for shifts in location if the shifts occurred when mother and pup were together. Our data suggest that a pup, if it becomes separated from its mother for a prolonged period, tends to remain at, or return to, the place where it was last suckled. Pup Number 4, for example, was apparently unattended by its mother from 14 to 20 June. During the period, it spent much of its time near one site, where eventually its mother found it. However, the pair was never observed suckling at this location again.

2) *Vocalization*: We assume that mother and pup learn to recognize each other's voices during the repeated vocal interchanges which begin immediately after birth and continue for several days thereafter. On scores of occasions we have watched females land at the rookery, stand with head high, trumpet the penetrating *pup-attraction call* and then move toward a nearby pod of pups. Usually a female will repeat the call several times per minute at irregular intervals. Typically, one of the pups in the vicinity responds to her call and moves directly toward her. Sometimes the pup is silent, but it usually replies with the bleat-like *mother-response call*, and then female and pup continue to vocalize alternately while moving

toward each other. Several pups sometimes approach a vocalizing female, but usually one is more vigorously responsive than the others. At night when we had crawled into a pod of sleeping pups, we several times saw individual pups suddenly rouse, reply to a distant pup-attraction call by uttering the mother-response call, and then move away to join the vocalizing female while the other pups in the pod remained sound asleep. The selectivity of response of both mothers and pups was impressive, particularly in August and September by which time the pups were 2–3 months old. Our observations left us convinced that vocal discrimination plays an important role in mother-young recognition.

3) *Vision*: Pups frequently respond positively to the sight of a female if holding her head high, particularly if she is walking out of the water onto the shore, and they may attempt to approach and nuzzle her even if no vocalization has occurred. This response is of low intensity and may occur simultaneously in several pups. Visual clues, although obviously used to orient female and pup toward each other, do not seem to contribute to specific individual identification. This is not surprising in view of the limited visual acuity of the species and in view of the fact that identification takes place at night as well as during the day.

4) *Olfaction*: From the frequency and persistence with which a female nuzzles and sniffs at her pup, we infer that olfactory information is important in close-range identification, as it seems to be in goats (Klopfer *et al.*, 1964). Once a female and pup have come together, they invariably touch noses and sniff at each other; this examination appears to complete the process of recognition. Without experimental evidence, we cannot say categorically that olfaction is the essential element in mutual recognition, but from field observation the case is convincing, particularly since the process frequently proceeds to the nuzzling stage before pups are rejected or accepted. We conclude that a female confirms the identification of her pup by its individual odor.

5) *Other clues*: Other possible sources of information that could be used for recognition are taste and touch. We cannot exclude these, since the female and pup rub whiskers and may touch each other's noses, but these sensory modalities do not appear to be of major importance.

SEASONAL CHANGES IN MOTHER-YOUNG RELATIONS.—As the summer progresses, pups and females spend progressively less time at the rookery where parturition occurred, and they seem to spend less time together on land. Since we often saw them depart together, and swim along near each other, it appears that increasing periods of time are spent together at sea during autumn months.

The mother-young tie may be maintained a year or longer. On 4 February 1950 on Islas San Benitos, Baja California, eight yearling-sized individuals were seen suckling, as were four others at San Nicolas Island on 23 April 1950, at a time when no pups had yet been born. During June and July 1965 we repeatedly observed suckling by individuals which could hardly have been less than one year old (Fig. 22), although we cannot exclude the possibility that these were young animals born out of season, in winter or spring.

We often saw young animals (yearlings) accompanying females at sea, swimming beside them and touching noses with them. On 15 July 1965 four female-yearling pairs were observed on land as part of an aggregation of animals which included no pups. One of the females moved away from the aggregation and the yearling followed, very much like a pup would. When the yearling crawled across the back of an adult, the two exchanged open-mouth threats, an interaction which was never seen between a pup and an adult. After moving 50 meters, the female lay down and the yearling began to suckle.

Yearling members of such pairs are very active and independent. For example, they will temporarily leave the adult and rush to the sea during a minor disturbance. Even while suckling, they are aggressive and may nip the mother or threaten her; they change teats frequently and the intervals of suckling seem to be short. We saw female-yearling pairs in both breeding and non-breeding aggregations. Presumably the yearlings are not exclusively dependent on their mothers for nutrition, but we have no data on this subject. Nor do we know if a female with a new pup continues to maintain ties with the offspring born in previous years.

Our observations on suckling in yearlings are not unique. Both Rowley (1929:18) and Orr (1965b:19) have previously reported instances of young *Zalophus* suckling long after they could reasonably be classified as pups.

FIG. 20. Pups play-fighting (top). The pup on the right has just lunged forward in a manner similar to that of a fighting bull.

FIG. 21. Female suckling pup on anterior teat (bottom).

Fɪɢ. 22. Female suckling a yearling

QUANTIFIABLE ASPECTS OF THE BIOLOGY OF ZALOPHUS

Population Dynamics

THE previous sections of this paper have developed a qualitative picture of the behavior of *Zalophus* and we can now attempt to quantify some aspects of its biology.

POPULATION FLUCTUATIONS.—The population of sea lions on San Nicolas Island during the breeding season remains in a state of flux. Individual adult males arrive from and depart for their non-breeding range at various times; pregnant females arrive at different times; some of the animals are always out at sea; bulls establish territories for a week or two then abandon them; pups are added in large numbers; animals change from one rookery to another or shift between hauling ground and rookery. Consequently, population estimates based on numbers of animals on shore on a given day do little more than indicate a lower limit for the total population.

The details of the distribution and numbers of *Zalophus* present on San Nicolas Island during the 1965 breeding season are shown in Table 1 and Figures 23 and 24. From May through September the population of adult females fluctuated between 2700 and 4200, but the number of territorial bulls never exceeded 408, and the number of non-breeders varied between 1600 and 2600. The maximum number of pups were present on shore during early July and since their population at this time was a little over 3600, there were at least 3600 breeding females based on the island during the breeding season. The total population, excluding pups, varied between 4100 and 5900. These last figures are more than twice those for the summer of 1949 (Bartholomew, 1951) but only slightly larger than those for the summer of 1958 (Bartholomew and Boolootian, 1960).

The relative changes in numbers in the different age and sex classes (Fig. 24) present on San Nicolas Island during the summer

45

TABLE 1

POPULATIONS OF *Zalophus californianus* ON SAN NICOLAS ISLAND, CALIFORNIA, DURING AND AFTER THE BREEDING SEASON OF 1965
SEE FIGURE 23 FOR LOCALITIES

Date	Class	Localities											Total
		1A	1B	2A	2B	3A	3B	4A	4B	4C	6A	6B	
1–4 June	Territorial bulls	210	21	10	30	25	28	0	4	7	3	70	408
	Breeding adult females	1080	190	325	40	350	250	100	30	48	25	290	2728
	Non-breeders	420	10	55	0	50	730	310	0	0	0	1050	2645
	Total adults	1710	221	390	70	425	1028	410	34	55	28	1410	5781
	Pups	980	46	200	300	280	225	27	20	31	20	230	2359
4–6 July	Territorial bulls	171	3	2	19	30	24	3	2	5	7	49	315
	Breeding adult females	1930	105	275	53	300	285	90	28	74	20	507	3667
	Non-breeders	485	0	150	20	34	250	550	0	0	0	300	1789
	Total adults	2586	108	427	92	364	559	643	30	79	27	856	5771
	Pups	2124	120	200	46	320	290	11	20	31	22	420	3604
2 Aug.	Territorial bulls	17	0	4	11	11*		0	0	0	3	10	56
	Breeding adult females	1150	0	190	65	780		10	0	350	38	620	3203
	Non-breeders	365	20	10	10	168		200	0	20	0	118	911
	Total adults	1532	20	204	86	959		210	0	370	41	748	4170
	Pups	1555	0	186	42	564		150	0	260	5	407	3015
14 Sept.	Territorial bulls		8*	14*		17*		0	4	2	1	20	66
	Breeding adult females	1265		870		1030		20	150	460	20	450	4265
	Non-breeders	750		85		40		370	0	150	0	200	1595
	Total adults	2023		969		1087		390	154	612	21	670	5926
	Pups	1195		640		790		0	135	340	52	340	3492

* Totals for adjacent localities combined.

of 1965 are consistent with what is known of seasonal changes in behavior and distribution of the *Zalophus* of the coasts of California and Baja California. Most of the pups were born during May and June and the increase in numbers of pups during early summer was merely an expression of the rate at which they were being added to the population. During July the number of pups present on the island decreased, presumably because of deaths and because the pups were spending progressively more time at sea as they grew older. The increase in pups during September is probably too great to be accounted for by sampling error and may indicate that pups born on other islands had followed their mothers to San Nicolas. The *Zalophus* population on San Nicolas is larger in winter than in summer (Bartholomew and Boolootian, 1960:368) and it is reasonable to assume that the increase in all classes of animals, except territorial bulls, that occurred during late summer was a result of an influx of animals that were elsewhere during the breeding season. The decrease in the number of territorial bulls in late summer coincides with, and may be related to, the arrival in late July and early August of a large contingent of male *Zalophus* at Año Nuevo Island, which lies 250 miles north of San Nicolas and which supports a very large population of male *Zalophus* during fall and winter (Orr and Poulter, 1965:394).

The short-term fluctuations of the numbers of *Zalophus* on San Nicolas during the summer are relatively small and resemble those of *Arctocephalus gazella* (Paulian, 1964:34) more than those of *Callorhinus* (Peterson, 1965b:20). Perhaps this is because *Zalophus* and *A. gazella* feed closer to their breeding grounds than does *Callorhinus*.

CHANGES IN LOCAL DISTRIBUTION.—Although the size of the sea lion population on San Nicolas as a whole remained relatively stable from day to day, the number of sea lions on any one rookery showed erratic short-term variations. This is shown by the periodic censuses of the various rookeries (Table 1) and particularly by the daily censuses of the study area (Table 2). Since we had many marked individuals in the study area we know that the fluctuations in animals there were caused by animals moving temporarily to other nearby areas as well as by their going to sea. It is obvious that because of the lack of close geographic ties, counts of a re-

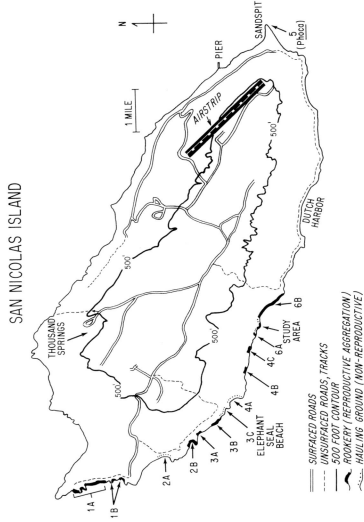

Fig. 23. Map of San Nicolas Island, California, showing location of pinniped rookeries and hauling grounds. The numbers of animals at the different localities are given in Table 1.

stricted area give little insight into the performance of the population of the island as a whole.

MORTALITY ON LAND.—We found few carcasses of pups or adults on land at any season. Since *Zalophus* stay very close to the water during the breeding season, it is possible that some pup carcasses wash to sea soon after death, which complicates any estimate of mortality. However, the mortality rate of pups on land appeared to us to be much less than that of *Callorhinus* on the Pribilof Islands, which ranges between 5 and 16 per cent during the breeding season (North Pacific Fur Seal Commission, 1962:5). For example, by 24 July 1965 only ten dead pups had been observed during the previous six weeks in an area where approximately 250 pups had been born.

On San Nicolas during the 1965 breeding season, natural mortality of adults on land was negligible. Several of the carcasses of adults which appeared on the beaches of San Nicolas showed signs of human predation: buckshot wounds, or evidence of clubbing or stoning.

Behavior of Individuals

TERRITORIAL BULLS.—By using scars and wounds for identification, we were able to recognize and follow from day to day 14 individual bulls in the study area. Although we accumulated many partial records, we had difficulty in obtaining satisfactorily complete data on length of territory maintenance; scar patterns disappeared or were altered, and bulls remained partly submerged in the water during daylight, making marks difficult to see. Five reliable and complete records of duration of territory maintenance were obtained during June and July. The mean duration was 9 days (3, 9, 9, 11, and 14 days). Our other records, although incomplete, suggest that these data are typical.

We have no evidence that individual bulls changed from one territory to another and we think that a given bull rarely assumes territorial status more than once during the season. However, in one instance a bull, marked by a projectile syringe in its flank, moved from a territory in Area 1B to a hauling ground on July 14, and later came back to his original territory.

ADULT FEMALES.—Despite a fairly good technique for marking females, we found difficulty in obtaining long serial records on them

TABLE 2

POPULATION OF *Zalophus* IN STUDY AREA DURING AND AFTER 1965 BREEDING SEASON

Date		Territorial bulls	Breeding adult females	Pups	Females per bull	Date		Territorial bulls	Breeding adult females	Pups	Females per bull
June	3	3	39	40	13.0	July	3	3	*	30	
	5	3	33	35	11.0		4	3	41	44	13.7
	6	4	*	29			5	3	38	47	12.7
	7	4	*	28			6	3	37	44	12.3
	8	3	48	33	16.0		7	3	43	41	14.3
	9	3	51	34	17.0		8	3	31	36	10.3
	10	3	46	32	15.3		9	2	*	38	
	11	2	47	20	23.5		12	2	29	40	14.5
	12	2	*	26			13	2	21	29	10.5
	14	2	38	20	19.0		14	2	28	22	14.0
	15	2	*	18			15	1	30	25	30.0
	16	2	*	*			17	2	38	22	19.0
	17	2	20	19	10.0		18	2	19	23	9.5
	19	4	43	48	10.8		20	2	15	26	7.5
	20	3	37	33	12.3		22	0	20	8	–
	21	4	39	40	9.8		24	2	32	20	16.0
	22	4	31	21	7.8		27	2	19	21	9.5
	24	4	36	30	9.0		28	1	24	9	24.0
	27	2	40	32	20.0		29	1	25	11	25.0
	28	2	56	37	28.0						
	29	2	52	51	26.0						
						Aug.	4	1	31	12	31.0
							5	1	37	15	37.0
							9	0	12	14	–
							10	0	26	21	–
							20	0	19	23	–
							21	0	7	17	–
							22	1	4	10	4.0
						Sept.	14	0	12	19	–
							15	1	21	26	10.5
							16	1	17	20	8.5

* Census incomplete.

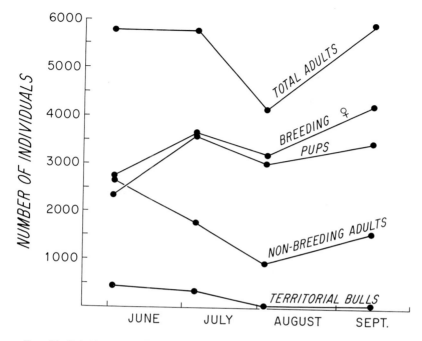

F<small>IG</small>. 24. *Zalophus* populations on San Nicolas Island during and after the 1965 breeding season. See Table 1 for a more detailed analysis.

because their extreme gregariousness made the marked animals hard to find and because they frequently changed locations in the rookery. Eight females with pups were marked and followed for approximately two months. To facilitate the assessment of the proportion of the time devoted to various activities, a marked female was arbitrarily assumed to have been in residence for all of each day on which she was seen in the study area.

The eight marked females were seen on shore in the study area an average of 34 per cent of the days under observation, and were seen suckling their pups on an average of 75 per cent of the days they were known to be on shore (Table 3). However, the amount of time spent on shore and the number of days on which they were seen suckling changed as the season advanced. During mid-June, when the pups were new, the females were on land an average of 50 per cent of the time, but thereafter the mean percentage de-

TABLE 3

SUMMARY OF RECORDS FOR 8 MARKED FEMALES OVER A TWO-MONTH PERIOD
DURING THE 1965 BREEDING SEASON

Female	Days of search	Days ob-served	Fraction of days present in study area	Days observed suckling	Fraction of days suckling
A	24	9	0.38	3	0.33
B	25	10	0.40	9	0.90
C	26	12	0.46	11	0.92
D	29	11	0.38	10	0.91
E	24	11	0.46	10	0.91
F	18	5	0.28	3	0.60
G	36	5	0.14	3	0.60
H	30	6	0.20	5	0.83
			$\overline{X}$ 0.34		$\overline{X}$ 0.75

creased markedly (Fig. 25). The proportion of days on which they suckled their pups declined sharply during July (Fig. 26).

PARTURITION AND COPULATION.—From the population curves (Fig. 24), it appears that most of the pups were born during June. However, females that were obviously pregnant were common at the study area from late May until about 10 July. More accurate data on the temporal pattern of parturition will require observations in April and May and more extensive population estimates.

The first copulation we observed was on 16 June, and thereafter copulation became progressively more common until the second week of July. By 22 July, the number of sexually responsive females had declined sharply as had the number of territorial bulls.

One marked female delivered during the night of 14 June and subsequently came into estrus 15 days later, on 29 June. To judge from this case, and the more general behavioral changes described above, we infer that estrus occurs approximately two weeks post partum. This period is similar to that in many other pinnipeds (Harrison *et al.*, 1952:439), but much longer than in *Callorhinus* (Bartholomew and Hoel, 1953:420).

PUPS.—The behavior of the 39 marked pups was classified in the same way as that of females. Six pups were observed on fewer than five days; 19 others were observed more often than this but were seen to be suckled on fewer than three days; while the other 14 were

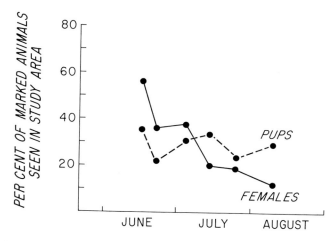

F_IG_. 25. Changes in the populations of 8 marked females and 39 pups in the study area. See also Tables 3 and 4.

seen more than five days and were suckled on more than three. These figures suggest that fewer than half the pups caught and marked at one rookery were actually resident, in the sense of being permanently based there and being suckled there frequently.

Excluding the group of six pups seen fewer than five times, on the average the marked pups were seen in the study area on 42 per cent of the days, and on 22 per cent of the days on land they were suckled. Considering only the 14 resident individuals, the comparable figures are 45 and 34 per cent, respectively.

The fraction of pups on land remained near the same level throughout the season (Fig. 25). Of the pups marked in early June, about one-third were observed in the study area on any subsequent day through early August. The percentage for resident pups was somewhat higher than that of the non-residents. The fraction of the days on which the marked pups were seen being suckled decreased from a mean of 56 per cent in mid-June to about 15 per cent in late June and to almost zero in August (Fig. 26).

P_ATTERNS_ _OF_ T_IMING_.—The data on time on land suggest that females do not remain separate from their pups either for extended or regular periods. Comparison of records of one female and her marked, resident pup (Table 4) indicates synchronous timing of

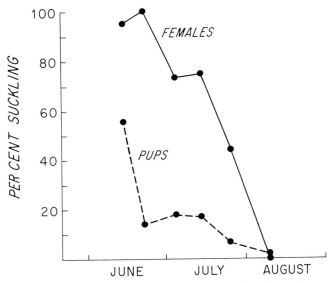

FIG. 26. Changes in amount of suckling by marked females and pups in the study area. See also Table 3.

behavior. The pup was observed on more days than was its mother, but it did not remain in the study area rookery continually. The intervals between the female's visits to the rookery varied from one to four days with no regular periodicity. The same statements apply to other resident pups and to the adult females.

In summary, a pup appears to be suckled at irregular intervals, which lengthen throughout the summer. Between times of suckling, both female and pup are concurrently absent from the rookery for considerable periods, particularly after the first ten days to two weeks post partum. The possibility exists that the pair may remain together elsewhere. This pattern contrasts sharply with the prolonged suckling broken by long, regular intervals of separation, as found in *Callorhinus* (Bartholomew and Hoel, 1953:421).

RATIO OF BREEDING FEMALES TO BREEDING MALES.—The unexpectedly low level of site tenacity in *Zalophus* makes it difficult to arrive at a satisfactory estimate of the effective sex ratio on the rookery. The aggregations of females are not harems in the sense of being groups controlled and maintained by the activities of the

TABLE 4

RECORDS OF OCCURRENCE OF A MARKED FEMALE AND HER MARKED PUP IN THE
STUDY AREA ON SAN NICOLAS ISLAND DURING CENSUSES ON 28 DIFFERENT DAYS
BETWEEN 13 JUNE AND 7 AUGUST 1965

	Days	% of days of observation
Female seen	10	36
Female seen with pup	10	36
Female seen without pup	0	0
Pup seen	15	54
Pup seen without female	5	18

territorial bulls. The females and pups shift from territory to territory and may even alternate between different rookeries. The females spend part of their time at sea. All of the females are not in the same reproductive condition at a given time, nor do individual bulls remain on territory throughout the breeding season. Consequently the raw census data shown in Tables 1 and 2 offer only a rough index to the effective sex ratio.

The degree of polygyny in this species can be best appraised if we can estimate the mean number of estrous females available to each territorial bull. Unfortunately, because of factors listed above, we can hope to achieve no more than rough approximations of upper and lower limits for the number of females per territorial bull (F_{TB}) during the month when breeding was at its peak (15 June to 15 July).

As shown in Table 1, at least 3604 pups were born on San Nicolas during the 1965 breeding season. This means that a minimum of 3600 parous females must have come into estrous during the breeding season. To this figure we can add at least 500 as a conservative estimate of the number of nulliparous females coming into estrous. The population of territorial bulls on the island during the breeding season averaged about 320. If we were to assume that each territorial male remained on his territory for the full 30 days, $F_{TB} = \dfrac{4100}{320} \cong 13$. However, we know from our study area data that the males remained on territory for about 9 days. Therefore, approximately 1060 of them would have occupied territories during the breeding season. Using these figures, $F_{TB} = \dfrac{4100}{1060} \cong 4$. From these computations we can conclude that on the island as a whole the ratio of estrous females to territorial bulls during the peak breeding month was at least $4 : 1$ and could hardly have exceeded $13 : 1$.

As a check of the rough calculations based on the total *Zalophus* population on San Nicolas, we can consider the small population in the study area which was under almost continuous scrutiny and for which we have relatively detailed information. Crude estimates of F_{TB} in this small sample during the peak of the breeding season can be made if we assume that during this period (15 June to 15 July) the rate at which females came into estrous remained constant and we know the following:

    a. The daily mean of the number of estrous females (14).
    b. The mean fraction of time the females stayed on the rookery (0.3).
    c. The length of the peak of the breeding season (30 days).
    d. The mean duration of territory maintenance by bulls (9 days).
    e. The daily mean of the number of territorial bulls (3).

A consideration of the assumptions and data enumerated above shows that $F_{TB} = \left(\dfrac{a}{b}\right) \div \left(\dfrac{c}{d} \times e\right) \cong 5$, which is similar to the minimum possible figure obtained using the population as a whole. F_{TB} can be calculated for the study area using the pups as an index to the number of estrous females. If we assume that the same number of pups entered the study area as left it, approximately 48 pups were born in the study area. If there were 48 pups, there were 48 parous estrous females, and we can add to these an estimate of 5 nulliparous estrous females. If the mean number of bulls was 3 and the average stay on territory was 9 days, there were 10 bulls present during this period. Using these figures, $F_{TB} \cong 5$ which approximates the minimum figure obtained from the population as a whole. Just for completeness we can examine the uncorrected data in Tables 1 and 2. During the breeding season the ratio of females to territorial bulls varied from rookery to rookery and from time to time. In the first week of June, the mean F_{TB} for the island as a whole was 7; during early July it was 12. On the study area during June and early July, F_{TB} varied between 8 and 28, with a mean of 14.

From the several approaches above, we can do no more than conclude that the ratio of estrous females to territorial bulls during the 1965 breeding season could hardly have been less than 4 : 1 nor more than 14 : 1.

DISCUSSION

A LTHOUGH otariids having the major morphological adaptations for aquatic life shown by living forms have been in existence since at least the upper middle Miocene (Mitchell, 1962), many features of the social behavior of sea lions remain strikingly similar to those of terrestrial mammals. The particular pattern of social behavior shown by *Zalophus* appears to be determined by the interplay between gregariousness and aggressiveness on the one hand, and the behavioral and morphological adaptations associated with its amphibious mode of life on the other.

Gregariousness

Like other otariids, *Zalophus* are strongly gregarious when on land. Although the species has traditional hauling grounds which have been used for several decades at least, a local population may shift from one area to another during a single breeding season. Even with this mobility, *Zalophus* group themselves in crowded aggregations separated by extensive unoccupied areas. This suggests that the local crowding so characteristic of *Zalophus* rookeries and hauling grounds is not related to scarcity of suitable land habitat but rather to gregariousness.

Terrestrial gregariousness in a wide-ranging marine mammal should help to assure that breeding groups adequate for reproduction will occur. In the case of *Zalophus*, which is almost certainly monestrous and which has a brief period of estrus, access of the female to a breeding bull during one limited period per year requires some special behavioral adaptations, an obvious one of which is gregariousness.

Another obvious selective advantage favoring extreme gregariousness is that it increases the chance of detecting and escaping from terrestrial danger. The presence of large numbers of individuals, any one of which by dashing toward the water can alert several hundred others to possible danger, compensates for the limited visual and olfactory acuity of the individual animals.

Aggressiveness

Gregariousness and aggressiveness are not mutually exclusive behavioral attributes. Opportunities for intraspecific aggressive behavior are obviously abundant in gregarious forms because of the frequency of contacts between individuals. In *Zalophus,* as in many other highly gregarious mammals, patterns of intraspecific aggression are well developed and aggressive interactions contribute importantly to the social structure. Aggressive behavior is more developed during the breeding season than at other times, and during the breeding season it is more intense on the rookeries than on the hauling grounds. In general, the aggressiveness of young animals is less than that of the adults. Breeding females react aggressively but with relatively low intensity toward other females, toward adult males, toward juveniles of both sexes, and often toward pups other than their own. The aggressive activities of breeding males are much more intense than those of the females, but are focused primarily on other males (including juveniles).

Like other mammals (Matthews, 1964:30), *Zalophus* shows a graded series of aggressive activities, extending from ritualized movements and threats to savage fighting. Even during their most violent fights, *Zalophus* bulls employ highly stereotyped movements and postures. Consequently the various customary categories of aggressive behavior are often difficult to distinguish. The classification which follows has a large arbitrary component.

THREATS.—Both postural and vocal threats are frequently used in encounters between males, females, and young, including pups. These threats vary in intensity from vocal signals indicating location or territory occupancy, to actions which are preliminary to violent fights. The basic threat is an open-mouthed thrust of the head accompanied by a vocalization, the characteristics of which vary with age and sex. This generalized expression of aggressiveness is extremely common and may be used by disturbed adults, juveniles, or pups of either sex at any season and normally involves pairs of individuals. The most common cause of this threat is the disturbance caused by an animal moving into or through a crowded group. Usually the animal causing the disturbance merely moves aside or retreats a few feet when it is threatened, but it may threaten in return before continuing on its way. This threat usually marks the total extent of an aggressive encounter, but during the breeding season it is sometimes the prelude to a fight and in most cases an animal that threatens gives the impression of being prepared for such an eventuality.

FIGHTS.—Fights in which serious wounds are inflicted occur most often between males in relation to territorial establishment and maintenance. However, females that are immediately post partum may fight vigorously but they rarely inflict visible damage on each other. Interactions which employ many of the motor patterns of fighting are frequent among young non-breeding animals but these are of low intensity and appear to be play.

Because they are so spectacular, the fights of otariid males have been cited as the most violent that occur among mammals. Nevertheless, actual physical fighting occurs only under a limited set of circumstances. *Zalophus* bulls fight only when territory maintenance is involved. Bulls inflict nasty cuts and gashes, but we have never seen a fight result in death. Postural and vocal threats precede and are intermingled with attempts to inflict physical damage, and some of the motor patterns involved in actual fighting have become ritualized as described below.

RITUALIZED AGGRESSIVE BEHAVIOR.—A significant component of the aggressive behavior of *Zalophus* bulls is ritualized in that it consists of signals which do not of themselves serve as threats. The ritualized aggressive behavior of *Zalophus* conforms to the original usage of Huxley (1923) in that its evolutionary derivation appears to be separate from its information content (cf. Lorenz, 1964:48). This is shown with particular clarity by the stereotyped and formalized boundary ceremony which is frequently engaged in by bulls with adjacent territories. The vocalizing, head-shaking, neck-arching, falling-prostrate, and oblique-staring patterns of the ceremony appear to be mutually recognized expressions of social status and do not lead to fighting. Nevertheless, the individual elements of the ceremony resemble the motor patterns used during fights: (1) Head-shaking is much the same movement that territorial bulls use when violently seizing and shaking an opponent. (2) The falling-prostrate maneuver is very similar to the forward lunge with protective appression of the foreflippers used by fighting territorial bulls. (3) The recurved-neck posture resembles a posture frequently seen during pauses between slashing bites. (4) The vocalizations used during ceremonies suggest prolonged versions of the grunts and gasps of fighting animals.

In the absence of information on sea lions reared in isolation, we cannot say whether these ritualized patterns are genetic or learned, but the individual behavioral elements appear early in ontogeny. Whatever the mode of transmission and maintenance, the motor elements in the boundary ceremony closely resemble, and appear to have been derived from, behavior used in fighting, and represent examples of ritualized behavior in the sense of Huxley (but not necessarily in the sense of Blest, 1961).

ONTOGENY OF AGGRESSIVE BEHAVIOR.—The precociousness of sea lion pups, and the ease with which the behavior of animals of all ages and both sexes can be observed at hauling grounds, allows the ontogeny of aggressive behavior to be followed from infant to adult with unusual clarity. The mock-battles of pups employ motor patterns which clearly anticipate, in an unorganized way, modes of aggressive expression used by adults. The prolonged, energetic games of juveniles (aged one to five years) closely resemble the serious threatening and fighting of adults, but the patterns are still incompletely developed and appear unrelated to any immediate goal other than play. Adult males on hauling grounds interact almost exactly like territorial bulls, although less intensively. Thus, the maturing sea lion continually refines and standardizes the motor patterns of aggressive expression.

Although these behavior patterns are performed frequently over a period of years, they are actually play until the individual becomes an effective member of the breeding population. In sea lions as in the polecats (*Mustela putorius*) described by Poole (1966), aggressive play consists of many activities that, in another context, are vital to reproduction and hence extremely important to survival. The transition from aggressive play to serious aggression is extremely subtle. For example, a bull when moving into a rookery merely performs, with heightened intensity and persistence, behavior patterns which, only a short time before, he may have been performing playfully on the hauling ground. But as soon as he enters a rookery, these patterns of behavior determine whether or not he will establish a territory and become part of the breeding population.

The motor patterns of play and serious aggression are so similar that in some circumstances we were unable to tell whether animals employing them were playing or not, and sometimes one member of a pair of participating animals may itself apparently briefly misinterpret the situation; i.e., one member of an interacting pair reacts playfully but the other reacts in a seriously aggressive manner. It seems that even though the motor patterns involved in social interaction appear to require several years of practice before they are performed accurately enough for them to have communicatory precision, the information content of even an accurate motor performance may be obscured except in the proper context.

EFFECTS OF AGGRESSIVENESS ON SOCIAL ORGANIZATION.—In *Zalophus* the spatial organization and structure of the adult breeding population are determined by aggressive interactions between individuals of the same sex. The interactions between females determine their location and spacing; the interactions between males determine whether they can come ashore in the vicinity of the females and also fix their location and spacing once they are ashore.

Aggressive interactions also support the integrity of mother-young pairs. Females prevent their newborn pups from coming into contact with other females by maintaining territories around themselves and by vigorously rebuffing any pup but their own which approaches. The pups at first appear to be attracted to any female, but the aggressiveness which they evoke from all females except their own mother strongly encourages them to react in a highly selective manner to the scores of females they encounter. This situation must contribute to the rapid development of the mutual recognition of mother and pup which is a basic component of the social pattern in *Zalophus*.

The extreme development of male secondary sexual characteristics in *Zalophus* is related to aggressiveness. The participation of a bull in reproductive activity depends upon his success in aggressive encounters with other bulls, since these encounters determine access to the females. Large size, thick neck pelage, and enlarged canines obviously enhance success in fighting, and so a condition exists which strongly favors the evolution and maintenance of these attributes (see Evolution of the Social System).

The territorial bulls show no aggressive reactions to pups, but their large size and rapid movements are an important source of potential danger to the pups. After they are a few weeks old the pups avoid active bulls. This has the effect of concentrating the pup pods in parts of the rookery where territorial activity is minimal and so contributes to the spatial organization of the rookeries.

During the non-breeding season when aggressiveness is greatly reduced, spatial organization is almost completely random, and the aggregations have no stable structure. The low intensity, non-reproductive aggressive interactions which are so common on the hauling grounds appear to contribute to comfortable spacing. Sea lions tend to form closely packed groups, and mildly aggressive reactions simply keep the degree of crowding to acceptable levels.

SUPPRESSION OF AGGRESSIVE BEHAVIOR.—During the breeding season, nearly all interactions between adult *Zalophus* have aggressive components and at least some of these must be suppressed for a stable social structure to persist, and for reproduction to be successful. Gregariousness balances the centrifugal effects of aggressiveness, but for successful copulation or for suckling, individuals must become at least temporarily tolerant of, or submissive to, others. As would be expected, therefore, there are two circumstances in which the usually aggressive reactions of *Zalophus* females are clearly suppressed; when they seek out and suckle their own pups, and when they actively solicit the attentions of and then copulate with a sexually active male.

Territorial bulls never suppress their aggressive behavior completely. Even during courtship and copulation they often vigorously threaten and nip at their partners. The acceptance by bulls of ritualized signals in place of fighting at territorial boundaries may be an example of partial suppression of overt aggression.

Amphibious Adaptations

Although California sea lions spend much of their time on shore their adaptations for aquatic life profoundly influence their social behavior. They are essentially coastal animals. Large populations can be found on shore at all times of the year. During the breeding season they appear to have obligatory ties to land; there is no evidence that the young can be successfully born and suckled at sea. Copulation is usually terrestrial, but aquatic copulations occur with some frequency so this aspect of reproduction does not have to be terrestrial.

LIMITED TERRESTRIAL MOBILITY.—In pinnipeds the stability of the social structure during the breeding season appears to be strongly affected by their limited terrestrial mobility, which, together with their sedentariness, allows many highly aggressive males to remain physically close to each other without disruptive interactions. For example, in those groups of northern elephant seals, *Mirounga angustirostris*, which happen to breed on narrow beaches, the ordinarily stable social structure often becomes chaotic at high tide when some of the females are partly awash (Bartholomew, 1952: 415). In this situation, the dominant male who is tied to the land cannot move rapidly enough to prevent the subordinate males that are swimming in the water from making rapid and repeated sorties into his harem. As a result the social structure temporarily disintegrates into a confused mélange of aggressive and sexual behavior.

By analogy with this situation, it seems possible that the looseness of the social structure in *Zalophus* as compared with *Callorhinus* may be associated with the close association of its rookeries with water. For example, in *Zalophus*, but not in *Callorhinus*, the male territories nearly always abut on the water; the females remain near the water's edge; aquatic copulations are common; and aggressive interactions between territorial bulls and males in the water are so frequent that the social structure is subjected to repeated disruptive influences.

SPECIAL SENSES.—Pinnipeds are faced with the difficult problem of obtaining adequate sensory information from both air and water— media with very different physical qualities. Judging by behavioral criteria, visual acuity of *Zalophus* in air is limited both at close range and at a distance. As previously described, only large moving objects evoke responses and none of the social signals they employ requires precise visual discrimination.

Although pinnipeds probably do not use olfactory clues underwater, during the terrestrial phases of their behavior *Zalophus* employ olfaction in at least two circumstances; in mother-young recognition and in identification of estrous females by bulls.

The marked development and conspicuous mobility of their vibrissae suggest that tactile information is important to *Zalophus*.

Certainly this is the case in social interactions on land—nuzzling and nose rubbing are conspicuous in contacts between pairs or groups of individuals.

Airborne acoustic signals are the primary means of social communication in *Zalophus*. We know of no other mammal which vocalizes as loudly and continuously as male *Zalophus,* and the females and pups are almost as vocal as the males. By means of vocal signals bulls indicate their identity, status, location, and aggressive intent; females summon and recognize their pups and express their aggressiveness; pups reply to their mothers and signal to each other. The overwhelming emphasis on acoustic signals is probably related to the specialization of the other special senses for underwater function. Vocal signaling also compensates in part for the limited terrestrial mobility because it permits the animals to communicate over considerable distances.

THERMOREGULATORY REQUIREMENTS.—Because of their amphibious mode of life, pinnipeds are faced with conflicting thermoregulatory needs. They must retain heat while in the water, but must be able to lose it while on land (Bartholomew and Wilke, 1956; Irving *et al.,* 1962). The conflicting demands for heat retention in water and heat dissipation in air are particularly acute for *Zalophus* because their warm-temperate and tropical distribution imposes a severe heat load on them when they are on shore. They have a low thermal conductance because of their large size and thick layer of subcutaneous fat. Consequently they face problems of overheating when they are active on land, especially in direct sunlight. They meet this probably in part by keeping wetted, thus taking advantage of evaporative cooling, and partly by staying on a wet substratum to which they readily lose heat by conduction. It seems likely that the thermoregulatory necessity for staying wet has been an important selective factor favoring partly aquatic territories. As discussed above, this has in turn affected the entire pattern of the reproductive behavior in this genus. In addition, the high level of nocturnal activity in *Zalophus* may be related to the avoidance of overheating.

EFFECTS OF HUMAN DISTURBANCE.—On the islands where they come ashore at the present time, *Zalophus* have no important enemies except man. Human disturbance has frequently driven other shore-breeding marine mammals nearly to extinction (*Callorhinus,*

Enhydra, Mirounga, Arctocephalus) or caused them to abandon their hauling grounds (for example, *Eumetopias* in the Pribilofs, Kenyon, 1962). Yet, some of the islands utilized by *Zalophus* have been occupied by Indians for several millenia (Meighan and Eberhart, 1953; Hubbs and Roden, 1964), and occupation of them by man continues at the present time.

Although in the Channel Islands *Zalophus* appear to prefer windward shores with extensive rocky shelves, they also use sandy beaches, sheltered cobble beaches, and even talus at the base of rocky cliffs for rookeries. Furthermore, site tenacity in *Zalophus* is limited and contrasts sharply with the remarkably conservative pattern of *Callorhinus* (Peterson, 1965*b*:93, 121). Even the breeding population of *Zalophus* is mobile. If harassed by humans or disturbed by storms, scores of animals may abandon a beach and move to nearby areas and there reconstitute their social structure. Females and pups move as pairs, by sea or overland, and a day or two after the females leave, the bulls abandon their territories. Other bulls, meanwhile, have established territories in the areas newly occupied by the females. These shifts may be local and temporary, or wide-spread and prolonged: we observed the temporary movement of one population as a result of our attempts to mark some individuals; and military operations have disturbed San Nicolas Area 1 so that during the past ten years the population there has gradually diminished despite a total increase in the island's population.

This lack of restrictive site attachment appears to have contributed to the success of *Zalophus* in the face of disturbance by modern man, but we do not believe that *Zalophus* could withstand excessive, widespread exploitation, or that incidental disturbance is harmless. The human population of California is competing increasingly with *Zalophus*, and protection of their rookeries will be necessary for continued survival of this valuable biological resource.

Evolution of the Social System

As Nutting (1891) pointed out, the breeding patterns of pinnipeds can be arranged in a series ranging from monogamous, relatively solitary genera with little sexual dimorphism (*Phoca, Hydrurga*), to extremely polygynous, highly gregarious, and dimorphic genera (*Callorhinus, Arctocephalus*). Between these extremes are a variety of intermediates: semi-gregarious genera (*Leptonychotes, Monachus*), and others in which a harem system is partially developed (*Halichoerus, Cystophora*). The more polygynous species copulate on land while the more nearly monogamous ones do so in the water, and the breeding season tends to be more compressed in the polygynous forms (Bertram, 1940:127). The degree of aggressiveness between males, and gregariousness among females, generally parallels the degree of polygyny.

Sea lions (subfamily *Otariinae*) are generally assumed to belong at the highly polygynous end of this series. Possibly, this may be correct for *Eumetopias* (Mathisen *et al.*, 1962:470; Daetz, 1959), for *Otaria* (Hamilton, 1934; vaz Ferreira, 1961), and for the little-known *Neophoca* and *Phocarctos* (King, 1964), although more adequate data are needed for all of these genera. *Zalophus,* however, can hardly be classified as one of the highly polygynous pinnipeds: copulation is frequently aquatic, females aggregate without regard to the territorial activity of bulls, male aggressiveness is relatively reduced and territories are held only briefly (actually less than the interval between parturition and estrous), temporary residence in the rookery by non-breeding males is common, and the breeding season is relatively prolonged. Admittedly, sexual dimorphism is conspicuous and females far outnumber males on the rookeries (a point to which we shall return). The social pattern of *Zalophus* resembles that of *Halichoerus* in the eastern Atlantic, which is rather loose and in which the degree of polygyny is moderate—both frequently copulate in the water, bulls cannot hold females against their will, male territories are short-lived and transient, and the females are relatively independent and aggressive (Hewer, 1960). We suggest that these two species should be considered weakly polygynous and placed midway in the behavioral series.

A reasonable hypothesis for the origin of polygynous social structure in pinnipeds can be formulated from the ideas originated by Nutting (1891) and elaborated by Bertram (1940) and Bartholomew (1952). The social pattern of the polygynous pinnipeds could have evolved as a result of the production of a combination of interactions between (1) their amphibious habits, (2) the gregariousness of the females, (3) the aggressiveness of males during the period of sexual activity, and (4) a basic pattern of reproductive physiology similar to most mammals, which permitted the exclusion of some males from the breeding population. Breeding females tended to aggregate in crowded groups when on land while the males were attracted to the vicinity of the females but, being intolerant of each other, spaced themselves more widely. Thus, a local imbalance in the sex ratio developed. The competition between males for location among the females led to this imbalance being self reinforcing. It also led to a selection for the epigamic and epideictic characters favoring success in aggressive interactions and elaborate patterns of threat behavior. This distortion of the effective sex ratio and exaggeration of sexual dimorphism could continue only until it became so extreme as to prevent an adequate reproductive rate.

This model suggests a possible mechanism whereby the system may have evolved, but does not consider the functional advantages conferred by this system which must have favored its selection and maintenance over alternatives. Wynne-Edwards (1962:525) has postulated that both gregarious breeding and polygamy are homeostatic adaptations by which regulation of population size is achieved and over-exploitation of the environment avoided. Wynne-Edwards' theory has been considered in relation to pinniped colonial behavior by Coulson and Hickling (1964:509). We suggest that this polygynous breeding pattern may also have other selective advantages. For example, for a pinniped in which copulation is restricted to land where locomotion and communication are difficult, the polygynous system might well be advantageous simply as an efficient mechanism of re-uniting the sexes at the proper time each year. Thus, in a wide-ranging marine species of small total population size, maintenance of a *minimum* reproductive rate could be a problem, and colonialism and polygyny might have helped to obviate it.

Our present concern is to evaluate these hypotheses and theories, and relate them to the observed patterns of behavior of *Zalophus*. Is the flexible polygynous system of *Zalophus* a stage in the gradual progression toward a more rigid pattern like that of *Callorhinus*? Or does it represent an evolutionary regression of the harem system, as the animals gradually become more aquatic in their reproduction?

Bertram (1940:128), in reviewing the behavior of pinnipeds, has proposed that the relatively sketchy harem system in *Halichoerus* is vestigial, and that the ". . . truly polygynous habit, which in the past was the cause of the sexual disparity in size and behavior in this species, is now in the process of decay due to the growing incidence of aquatic copulation." The same logic is applicable to *Zalophus*. The alternative, that polygyny and its concomitant features are just beginning to evolve, is less tenable since morphologic dimorphism is much more highly developed in *Zalophus* than seems warranted by the present, loose social pattern.

Coulson (1965:55) objected to the idea that colonial breeding in grey seals is a vestigial behavior pattern, suggesting that if this behavior were not serving important functional purposes, it would rapidly disappear since "selection pressures against its persisting are high." We do not propose that *all* the selective advantages which once favored the evolution of colonial breeding, polygyny, and dimorphism have disappeared from the animals' present environment. Instead, we suggest that *some* of the advantages, to *Zalophus* and *Halichoerus* at least, may have been reduced, resulting in a partial regression of the harem system. An important factor contributing to the relaxing of the social structure may be the increase in frequency of aquatic copulation, which, as Bertram showed, could obviate much of the terrestrial social behavior of pinnipeds. Another potentially important factor for *Zalophus* is the relatively high temperature on their rookeries during the daytime, which apparently causes them to remain near the edge of the water. The high level of mobility of males in the water makes prolonged maintenance of territories abutting on the water difficult. (Even in *Callorhinus* such territories are unstable, Bartholomew, 1953.) The frequent visits of females to the edge of the water for thermoregulatory purposes impede the maintenance of stable harems and of course make possible aquatic copulations. It is noteworthy that in *Callorhinus* harem maintenance is relatively ineffective on the infrequent sunny days on which heat stress causes females to leave the rookery and enter the water (Bartholomew and Hoel, 1953; Bartholomew and Wilke, 1956).

SUMMARY

THIS study of the natural history and social behavior of the California sea lion
(*Zalophus californianus*) is based primarily
on observations made on San Nicolas Island,
California, during the spring and summer of
1965, but it draws on data acquired during
the past two decades on the islands off Cali-
fornia and Baja California and on the Galapagos Islands, Ecuador.

Zalophus are highly gregarious at all seasons. They are primarily
coastal in distribution and haul out on shore throughout the year.
Although their primary locomotor adaptations are for swimming,
with the primary propulsive force being supplied by simultaneous
strokes of the front flippers, they are capable of effective locomotion
on land. Their terrestrial locomotion is variable and includes
walking, galloping, and striding with front flippers only. Despite
their short pelage they groom themselves extensively using both
front and hind flippers and occasionally the teeth. They also often
rub themselves, particularly their snouts, against each other and
against inanimate objects. They have no special postures for defecation or urination.

While on shore they appear sensitive to high air temperatures and
direct solar radiation and on warm days remain on the wet sand
and rocks at the water's edge and frequently wet themselves down.

The visual acuity of *Zalophus* in air seems limited, but they
readily distinguish bold outlines and rapid movements. Auditory
and olfactory discrimination appear to be well developed.

Interspecific interactions with elephant seals, harbor seals, and a
variety of birds are common. *Zalophus* tend to be dominant in their
relations with harbor seals and young elephant seals, but not with
adults of the latter.

During the non-breeding season *Zalophus* appear to have no
stable social organization while on shore although there are obvious,
but presumably transient, size-related dominance relations. Except
during the breeding season there is a strong, although incomplete,
sexual allopatry. The adult males, but not the females or immature

animals, tend to move to or beyond the northern part of the breeding range.

During the non-breeding season the escape reaction of *Zalophus* is more pronounced than during the breeding season. At all seasons their alarm response is highly contagious and is often evoked by the alarm reaction of gulls associated with them.

Zalophus are highly polygynous seasonal (June and July) breeders. Only territorial bulls participate in the breeding structure. The male territories almost invariably abut on the water and some are completely aquatic. Bulls rarely hold territory continuously for more than two weeks so that a given territory may be occupied by a succession of bulls during the breeding season. The males establish and maintain their territories by aggressive behavior involving almost incessant vocalization, frequent threats, and sometimes violent fights. However, adjacent territorial bulls do not fight with each other, but maintain their status by stereotyped patterns of behavior apparently derived from the motor patterns of fighting. The females pay no attention to the boundaries of the male territories and move freely from territory to territory. The males do not attempt to hold the females so harems as such do not exist.

Although the females are extremely gregarious they are sufficiently aggressive toward each other immediately post partum that for a few days they are almost territorial. The females are monestrous and estrus occurs about two weeks post partum. Copulation usually takes place on land but it often occurs partly or completely in the water. Females apparently usually copulate only once during estrus.

Parturition usually occurs at night. The pups are extremely precocious and can locomote and vocalize within a few minutes of birth. Females are very solicitous of their pups for the first few days and maintain almost continuous contact with them. They take their pups with them when changing positions in the rookery, and when going into the water to cool off they sometimes drag the pups with them into the water. As the season progresses the females spend progressively less time with their pups.

By the time the pups are a couple of weeks old they aggregate into pods in the quieter parts of the rookery. They spend much time in play both on land and in the water. Their play anticipates many of the activities of the adults, particularly fighting and copulation. They spend progressively more time in the water as they become older.

Each female recognizes its own pup and suckles it to the exclusion of all others. Mother-pup recognition involves location by vocalization and final identification by olfaction. Visual clues appear to be of minor importance. Mother-young ties are sometimes maintained for a year or more and females are frequently seen nursing yearlings.

From May through September 1965, the population of adult females on San Nicolas Island fluctuated between 2700 and 4200, but the number of territorial bulls never exceeded 408. The total population on the island, excluding pups, fluctuated between 4100 and 5900. Slightly more than 3600 pups were born. Pup mortality was very low compared with that of other highly colonial pinnipeds.

The mean duration of territory maintenance of individually known bulls was 9 days and the longest was 14 days. The females appear to spend about one day in three ashore with their pups.

Various methods of calculating the ratio of breeding females to breeding males on the rookeries yield figures that indicate that the ratio can hardly be less than 4 : 1 or more than 14 : 1.

The particular pattern of social behavior shown by *Zalophus* appears to have been determined by the interplay between gregariousness and aggressiveness on the one hand and the behavioral and morphological adaptations associated with an amphibious mode of life on the other. The roles of each of these are discussed as are the relation of play to the ontogeny of aggressive behavior and factors contributing to the evolution and maintenance of the polygynous social structure of *Zalophus*.

Literature Cited

BARTHOLOMEW, G. A. 1951. Spring, summer and fall censuses of the pinnipeds on San Nicolas Island, California. Jour. Mamm., 32:15–21.

――――― 1952. Reproductive and social behavior of the northern elephant seal. Univ. Calif. Publ. Zool., 47:369–472.

――――― 1953. Behavioral factors affecting social structure in the Alaska fur seal. Trans. 18th N. Amer. Wildl. Conf., Pp. 481–502.

――――― 1959. Mother-young relations and the maturation of pup behaviour in the Alaska fur seal. Anim. Behav., 7:163–171.

BARTHOLOMEW, G. A., AND R. A. BOOLOOTIAN. 1960. Numbers and population structure of the pinnipeds on the California Channel Islands. Jour. Mamm., 41:366–375.

BARTHOLOMEW, G. A., AND N. E. COLLIAS. 1962. The role of vocalization in the social behaviour of the northern elephant seal. Anim. Behav., 10: 7–14.

BARTHOLOMEW, G. A., AND P. G. HOEL. 1953. Reproductive behavior of the Alaska fur seal, *Callorhinus ursinus*. Jour. Mamm., 34:417–436.

BARTHOLOMEW, G. A., AND C. L. HUBBS. 1952. Winter population of pinnipeds about Guadalupe, San Benito, and Cedros islands, Baja California. Jour. Mamm., 33:160–171.

BARTHOLOMEW, G. A., AND F. WILKE. 1956. Body temperature in the northern fur seal, *Callorhinus ursinus*. Jour. Mamm., 37:327–337.

BERING SEA TRIBUNAL OF ARBITRATION. 1895. Fur seal arbitration: Proceedings of the tribunal convened at Paris for the governments of the United States and Great Britain, for determination of questions between the two governments concerning jurisdictional rights to the waters of the Bering Sea. Washington, D. C. 53rd Congress, 2nd Session. Senate Ex. Doc. no. 177.

BERTRAM, G. C. L. 1940. The biology of the Weddell and crabeater seals, with a study of the comparative behaviour of the Pinnipedia. British Graham Land Exped., 1934–1937. Sci. Reps., 1:1–139.

BLEST, A. D. 1961. The concept of ritualisation, *In* Current problems in animal behaviour. W. H. Thorpe and O. L. Zangwill (Eds.). University Press, Cambridge, Pp. 102–124.

BONNOT, P. 1928. Report on the seals and sea lions of California. Fish. Bull. 14, Calif. Div. Fish and Game., 62 pp.

CARRICK, R., S. E. CSORDAS, AND S. E. INGHAM. 1962. Studies on the southern elephant seal, *Mirounga leonina* (L.) IV. Breeding and development. Commonwealth Sci. Ind. Res. Org. Wildl. Res., 7:161–197.

COLLIAS, N. E. 1956. The analysis of socialization in sheep and goats. Ecology, 37:228–239.

COULSON, J. C. 1965. Colonial breeding in grey seals, *In* A seals symposium. E. A. Smith (Ed.). The Nature Conservancy, Edinburgh, Scotland, Pp. 55–56.

COULSON, J. C., AND G. HICKLING. 1964. The breeding biology of the grey seal,

Halichoerus grypus (Fab.), on the Farne Islands, Northumberland. Jour. Anim. Ecol., 33:485–512.

DAETZ, G. M. 1959. Alaskan challengers of the sea. Nat. Hist., 68:334–347.

EIBL-EIBESFELDT, I. 1955. Ethologische Studien am Galapagos-Seelöwen, *Zalophus wollebaeki* Sivertsen. Zeit. f. Tierpsychol., 12:286–303. (English translation on file at Marine Mammal Biological Laboratory, Seattle.)

EVANS, W. E., AND R. M. HAUGEN. 1963. An experimental study of the echolocation ability of a California sea lion, *Zalophus californianus* (Lesson). Bull. So. Cal. Acad. Sci., 62:165–175.

FERREIRA, R. VAZ. 1961. Estructura de una agrupacion social reproductora de *Otaria byronia* (de Blainville), representacion grafica. Facultad de Humanidades y Ciencias, Dept. Zool. Vertebrados, Univ. Montevideo, Uruguay. Revista 19:253–260.

FISCUS, C. H., G. A. BAINES, AND F. WILKE. 1964. Pelagic fur seal investigations, Alaska waters, 1962. U. S. Fish and Wildl. Serv., Washington, D. C., Spec. Sci. Rep. Fish. 475, 59 pp.

FISCUS, C. H., AND G. A. BAINES. 1966. Food and feeding behavior of Steller and California sea lions. Jour. Mamm., 47:195–200.

FRY, D. H., JR. 1939. A winter influx of sea lions from Lower California. Calif. Fish and Game, 25:245–250.

HAMILTON, J. E. 1934. The southern sea lion, *Otaria byronia* (de Blainville). Discovery Reports, 8:269–318.

HARRISON, R. J., L. H. MATTHEWS, AND J. M. ROBERTS. 1952. Reproduction in some Pinnipedia. Trans. Zool. Soc. London, 27:437–540, 4 pls.

HEWER, H. R. 1960. Behaviour of the grey seal (*Halichoerus grypus* Fab.) in the breeding season. Mammalia, 24:400–421.

HILLINGER, C. 1958. The California Islands. Academy Publications, Los Angeles, California, 165 pp.

HOBSON, E. S. 1966. Visual orientation and feeding in seals and sea lions. Nature, 210:326–327.

HOWELL, A. B. 1930. Aquatic mammals, their adaptations to life in the water. Chas. C Thomas, Baltimore, 338 pp.

HUBBS, C. L., AND G. I. RODEN. 1964. Oceanography and marine life along the Pacific Coast of Middle America, *In* Vol. 1, Handbook of Middle American Indians, University of Texas Press, Pp. 143–186.

HUXLEY, J. S. 1923. Courtship activities in the red-throated diver (*Colymbus stellatus* Pontopp.); together with a discussion of the evolution of courtship in birds. Jour. Linn. Soc. Lond., 35:253–292, 2 pls.

IRVING, L., L. J. PEYTON, C. H. BAHN, AND R. S. PETERSON. 1962. Regulation of temperature in fur seals. Physiol. Zool., 35:275–284.

KENYON, K. W. 1956. The circus seal at home. Nat. Hist., 65:195–201.

———— 1960. Territorial behavior and homing in the Alaska fur seal. Mammalia, 24:432–444.

———— 1962. History of the Steller sea lion at the Pribilof Islands, Alaska. Jour. Mamm., 43:68–75.

KENYON, K. W., AND D. W. RICE. 1959. Life history of the Hawaiian monk seal. Pacific Science, 12:215–252.

KENYON, K. W., AND F. WILKE. 1953. Migration of the northern fur seal, *Callorhinus ursinus.* Jour. Mamm., 34:86–98.

KING, J. E. 1961. Notes on the pinnipedes from Japan described by Temminck in 1844. Zool. Mededelingen, 37:211–224, 5 pls.

——— 1964. Seals of the world. The British Museum (Natural History), London, 154 pp.

KLOPFER, P. H., D. K. ADAMS, AND M. S. KLOPFER. 1964. Maternal "imprinting" in goats. Proc. Nat. Acad. Sci., 52:911–914.

LAWS, R. M. 1956. The elephant seal (*Mirounga leonina,* Linn.) II. General, social and reproductive behaviour. Falkland Is. Dependencies Survey, London. Sci. Rept., 13, 88 pp.

LOIZOS, C. 1966. Play in mammals. Symp. Zool. Soc. London, 18:1–9.

LORENZ, K. 1964. Ritualized fighting, *In* The natural history of aggression. J. D. Carthy and F. J. Ebling (Eds.). Academic Press, New York, Pp. 39–50.

MARLER, P. 1963. Book review, The mountain gorilla: ecology and behavior, by G. B. Schaller. Science, 140:1081–1082.

MATTHEWS, L. H. 1964. Overt fighting in mammals, *In* The natural history of aggression. J. D. Carthy and F. J. Ebling (Eds.). Academic Press, New York, Pp. 23–32.

MATHISEN, O. A., R. T. BAADE, AND R. J. LOPP. 1962. Breeding habits, growth and stomach contents of the Steller sea lion in Alaska. Jour. Mamm., 43:469–477.

MEIGHAN, C. W., AND H. EBERHART. 1953. Archaeological resources of San Nicolas Island, California. Amer. Antiquity, 19:109–125.

MITCHELL, EDWARD D., JR. 1962. A walrus and a sea lion from the Pliocene purisma formation at Santa Cruz, California: with remarks on the type locality and geologic age of the sea lion *Dusignathus santacruzensis* Kellogg. Los Angeles County Mus. Contrib. in Sci. 56, 23 pp.

NORTH PACIFIC FUR SEAL COMMISSION, STANDING SCIENTIFIC COMMITTEE. 1962. Report on investigations from 1958 to 1961. Washington, D. C., 183 pp.

——— 1963. Glossary of terms used in fur seal research and management. U. S. Dept. Interior, Fish and Wildl. Serv., Washington, D. C. Fishery Leaflet 546, 9 pp.

NICE, M. M. 1962. Development of behavior in precocial birds. Trans. Linn. Soc. N. Y., 8:xii + 211.

NUTTING, C. C. 1891. Some of the causes and results of polygamy among the Pinnipedia. Amer. Naturalist, 25:103–112.

O'GORMAN, F. 1963. Observations on terrestrial locomotion in Antarctic seals. Proc. Zool. Soc. London, 141:837–850.

ORR, R. T. 1965a. Interspecific behavior among pinnipeds. Zeit. f. Säugetierkunde, 30:163–171.

——— 1965b. Barrington Island. California Monthly, 75 (10) :18–20.

ORR, R. T., AND T. C. POULTER. 1965. The pinniped population of Año Nuevo Island, California. Proc. Calif. Acad. Sciences, Fourth Series, 32:377–404.

PAULIAN, P. 1964. Contribution a l'etude de l'otarie de l'Ile Amsterdam. Mammalia, 28:1–146, 10 pls.

PETERSON, R. S. 1965a. Drugs for handling fur seals. Jour. Wildl. Mgt., 29: 688–693.

———— 1965b. Behavior of the northern fur seal. Dr. Sci. Thesis. Johns Hopkins University, Baltimore, Maryland, 214 pp.

POOLE, T. 1966. Aggressive play in polecats. Symp. Zool. Soc. London, 18:23–44.

POULTER, T. C. 1963. Sonar signals of the sea lion. Science, 139:753–755.

RAY, C. 1963. Locomotion in pinnipeds. Natural Hist., 72 (3) :10–21.

ROWLEY, J. 1929. Life history of the sea lions of the California coast. Jour. Mamm., 10:1–36.

SCAMMON, C. M. 1874. The marine mammals of the north-western coast of North America. John H. Carmany and Co., San Francisco, 319 pp.

SCHEFFER, V. B. 1958. Seals, sea lions and walruses. A review of the pinnipedia. Stanford University Press. 179 pp., 33 pls.

———— 1964. Hair patterns in seals (Pinnipedia). Jour. Morphol., 115:291–303.

SCHEFFER, V. B., AND J. A. NEFF. 1948. Food of California sea lions. Jour. Mamm., 29:67–68.

SCHUSTERMAN, R. J., AND S. N. FEINSTEIN. 1965. Shaping and discriminative control of underwater click vocalizations in a California sea lion. Science, 150:1743–1744.

SCHUSTERMAN, R. J., W. N. KELLOGG, AND C. E. RICE. 1965. Underwater visual discrimination by the California sea lion. Science, 147:1594–1596.

SHORT, R. V., AND J. M. KING. 1964. The design of a crossbow and dart for immobilisation of wild animals. Vet. Record, 76:628–630.

SLIJPER, E. J. 1956. Some remarks on gestation and birth in cetacea and other aquatic mammals. Hvalråd. Skr., 41:1–62.

SMITH, E. A. 1965. The effects of human interference in a grey seal breeding colony and the phenomenon of fosterage, *In* A seals symposium. E. A. Smith (Ed.). The Nature Conservancy, Edinburgh, Pp. 63–75.

SMITH, M. S. R. 1965. Weddell seals, *In* A seals symposium. E. A. Smith (Ed.). The Nature Conservancy, Edinburgh, Pp. 9–16.

STELLER, G. W. 1751. De bestiis marinis. Typis Academiae Scientiarum, Petropoli. Translation by W. Miller and J. E. Miller, *In* The fur seals and fur-seal islands of the North Pacific Ocean, Part 3. D. S. Jordan, *et al.* (Ed.), 1898. Govt. Print. Office, Washington, Pp. 179–218.

WALLS, G. L. 1942. The vertebrate eye and its adaptive radiation. Cranbrook Institute of Science, Bloomfield Hills, Michigan. Bull. No. 19, 785 pp.

WINSLOW, J. H. 1960. San Nicolas Island, Channel Islands, Ventura County, California, a library brochure. Prepared for Pacific Missile Range, Point Mugu, California, with the University of California. 62 pp. (Processed).

WYNNE-EDWARDS, V. C. 1962. Animal dispersion in relation to social behavior. Oliver and Boyd, Edinburgh, Scotland, 653 pp.

Accepted for publication August 15, 1966

Index